Universal Dinnerware and its Predecessors

CO 1 59 41201 C4

4880 Lower Valley Road, Atglen, PA 19310 USA

Dedication

This book is dedicated to all the past employees of the Universal Potteries, Inc. who labored and toiled. They are not around today but their efforts will forever be in print when our memories fade.

My only memories were of playing in the old pottery dump as a child, not realizing the impact it would have on my life.

I want to make a special dedication in memory of Eve Basford who sparked my interest in Universal Pottery and all other associated potteries.

Designed by "Sue"
Type set in Americana XBd BT/Souvenir Lt BT

ISBN: 0-7643-1036-4
Printed in China
1 2 3 4

Published by Schiffer Publishing Ltd.
4880 Lower Valley Road
Atglen, PA 19310
Phone: (610) 593-1777; Fax: (610) 593-2002
E-mail: Schifferbk@aol.com
Please visit our web site catalog at
www.schifferbooks.com

This book may be purchased from the publisher.
Include $3.95 for shipping.
Please try your bookstore first.
We are interested in hearing from authors
with book ideas on related subjects.
You may write for a free catalog.

In Europe, Schiffer books are distributed by
Bushwood Books
6 Marksbury Avenue
Kew Gardens
Surrey TW9 4JF England
Phone: 44 (0) 208 392-8585; Fax: 44 (0) 208 392-9876
E-mail: Bushwd@aol.com

Acknowledgments

Words cannot express the deep appreciation I have for all the people who have made this publication a reality. Without the support and interest of all of my friends, and my new friends—the employees of Universal Potteries, Inc.—I could not have completed this memorial to all those who labored so that collectors and families could say: "My father, or mother, made this with their own hands," and that collectors could enjoy the beauty of what was made in Cambridge, Guernsey County, Ohio.

I give special thanks to the following: Chester Wardeska, William McClelland, Pauline Aleshire, Fred Betts, Monna Rose, Albert Campbell, Richard Mayor, Arden Kail, Robert Gibson, Fred Betts, Bill Burgess, my nephew Robert (Red Dog) Collins, Lorraine Weinman, Anna Pavlov-Perez, and Fran & Dick Pavlov of Penny Court Antique Mall in Cambridge, Ohio. I apologize if anyone has been omitted; it was not intentional.

Contents

Introduction 4
Cambridge Art Pottery 5
The Guernsey Earthenware Co. 10
Oxford Pottery Co. 20
The Atlas-Globe China Co. 25
Universal Potteries, Inc. 34
Index 175

Introduction

I have collected Universal Dinnerware for a number of years. This, of course, grew rapidly into collecting from all of the past potteries that made up the Universal Pottery, Inc. I call it the "family tree" of Universal Potteries, Inc., which began in 1900 with Cambridge Art Pottery and ended in 1960 with the Universal Potteries, Inc.

This book illustrates examples of the many shapes and colors that span the sixty year history of potteries in Cambridge, Ohio. Did you eat from dinnerware with pictures of Roy Rogers and Trigger when you were a small child? These items were made by Universal with a rope border called Rodeo. You may not be familiar with the name Universal, but you may recognize shapes such as Rodeo, Ballerina, Mt. Vernon, and Fascination, and you may remember decorations like Cattail, Bittersweet, Circus, and Calico Fruit with its vivid blue and red plaid fruit. These are but a few of the popular decorations to spark the interest of the new collector. For this book, if the name of the shape or decoration was known, I have included it in the photo caption. Some names of shapes and decorations remain unknown at this time, however.

A great deal of time has been spent researching records, catalogs, magazines, and newspapers. I have had a glorious time reminiscing with pottery workers who shared their love of the pottery industry.

I have enjoyed the hunt and decided it is time to share with the world. While I have included as much last-minute data as possible, some information will unfortunately not be available in time. In hopes of preserving this history, I will continue to seek out information and encourage readers to add any they might care to share.

Cambridge Art Pottery

The Cambridge Art Pottery was formed in 1900 by Charles L. Casey, O.M. Hoge, A.M. Sarchet, A.J. McCullough, Frank Haws, and George Cunningham.

By August 1900, Charles L. Casey had been elected president; A.M. Sarchet, secretary; O.M. Hoge, treasurer; with George Cunningham and Frank Haws superintendents of the plant.

This plant produced beautiful art glazes comparable to Weller and Brush, although this was short-lived following the introduction in 1903 of its "Guernsey Ware" cooking utensils, which received first prize at the Jamestown Exposition of 1907.

The Cambridge Art Pottery was built near a rich clay deposit, thus lowering costs. Clay was in such abundance that it was sold to Paden City Iron & Pottery Company at seventy-five cents a ton.

Early production pieces offered were pedestals, umbrella stands, jardinieres, cuspidors, steins, and tankards.

In 1902, an artware line called "Terrhea" was introduced along with "Oakwood," "Acorn," and "Otoe."

Portrait vase, Cambridge Art Pottery. 10.25" h. $1200-1400.

Vase, Cambridge Art Pottery. 14.25" h. $1000-1100.

Vase, corn decoration, 12.5" h., $900-1100; mug, cherries decoration, 4" h. $200-225. Both made by the Cambridge Art Pottery.

Backstamp from bottom of the Cambridge Art Pottery mug.

Vase, Cambridge Art Pottery.
11.5" h. $275-300.

Vase, artist signed, Cambridge Art Pottery. 5.5" h., $250-275.

Three vases from the Cambridge Art Pottery. From left: 5.5" h., $225-275;
6" h., $200-225; 3" h., $175-200.

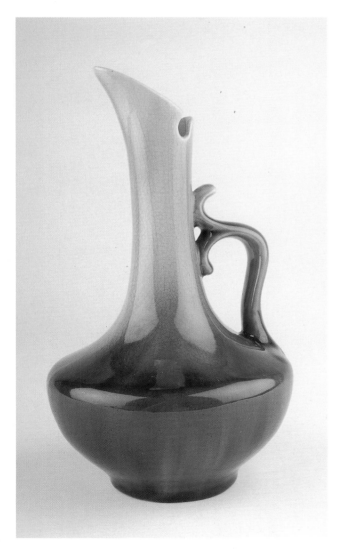

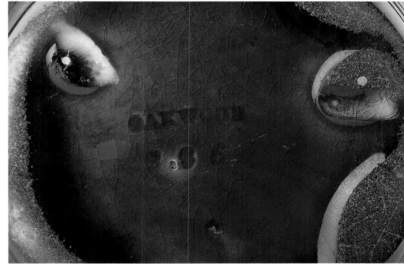

Backstamp from bottom of the Oakwood ewer at left.

Ewer, "Oakwood," Cambridge Art Pottery. 8" h.. $100-125.

The Guernsey Earthenware Co.

On May 27, 1909, the name of The Cambridge Art Pottery was changed to The Guernsey Earthenware Co.

In January 1909, an advertisement for the company offered "Guernsey Cooking Ware, ramekins, custard cups, cocottes, shirred egg and pudding dishes, pie plates, bowls, stew pots, tea and chocolate pots, casseroles and bean pots."

In 1914, the *Guernsey Times* (Guernsey County, Ohio) hailed them as "Largest Earthen Cooking Utensil manufacturers in the world."

A Hotel Ware line was added by the company in 1918 to supply government needs and shortages during World War I.

By 1923 the company name had again been changed to The Guernseyware Co. and later to the Guernseyware China Co. in 1924-25.

The Potter-Davis Company was a local distributor. In 1925, the Guernseyware China Co. passed from existence with its purchase on June 8 by the Globe China Company of Niles, Ohio.

Oval covered casserole with matching underplate, Cambridge Art Pottery/Guernsey Cooking Ware. 4" h. x 9.75" dia. $32-38.

Covered casserole (missing lid) with matching underplate, Cambridge Art Pottery/Guernsey Cooking Ware. 3.5" h. x 7.25" dia. $20-24.

Covered casserole, Cambridge Art Pottery/Guernsey Cooking Ware. 3.5" h. x 8.25" dia. $40-46.

Teapot and underplate, Cambridge Art Pottery/Guernsey Cooking Ware.
Teapot: 5.5" h., $20-24; underplate, 6" dia., $6-8.

Three pieces from the Cambridge Art Pottery/Guernsey Cooking
Ware. Teapot: 5.5" h., $45-50; creamer, 3" h., $8-12; chocolate
cup, 3.75" h., $10-16.

Backstamp from bottom of teapot shown at left.

Creamer and sugar, Cambridge Art Pottery/Guernsey Cooking
Ware. Creamer: 3.5" h., $14-16; sugar, 2.5" h., $8-12.

Tea set, Cambridge Art Pottery/Guernsey Cooking Ware. Teapot, 6.5" h.,
on 6" dia. underplate, $55-60; creamer, 3.25" h., $16-18; sugar, 4.5" h.,
$8-12.

Covered casserole, Cambridge Art Pottery/Guernsey Cooking Ware. 3.5" h. x 8.25" dia., with matching underplate, 9.75" dia. $32-38.

Cambridge Art Pottery/Guernsey Cooking Ware. Condiment jar, 1.75" h., $8-10; condiment jar in metal holder, 2.25" h., $10-12; assorted ramekins, 2.5" to 3.5" dia., $6-10 ea.

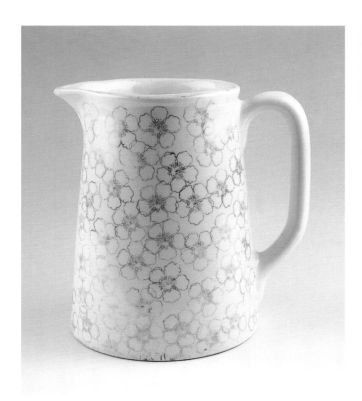

Milk pitcher, Cambridge Art Pottery/Guernsey Cooking Ware. 7.75" h., $24-26.

Cambridge Art Pottery/Guernsey Cooking Ware. Crock, 9" h. x 11.5" dia., $20-25; teapot, 4.75" h., $8-10; mixing bowl, 5.75" h. x 12" dia., $18-22.

Additional Cambridge Art Pottery/Guernsey Cooking Ware pieces. Spittoon, 4.25" h., $35-40; oval ramekin, 10.75" l., $10-16; custard cup, 2.5" h., $4-6; octagonal cup, 1.75" h., $6-8.

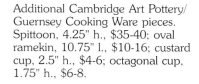

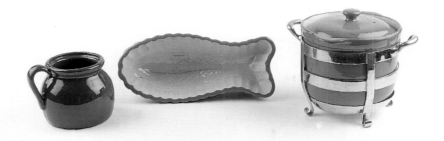

Guernsey Cooking Ware. Brown glazed bean pot (missing lid), 4" h., $8-10; fish mold, 10" l., $40-45; redware bean pot with lid and metal holder, 5.5" h., $20-22.

Mark on bottom of the Guernsey Ware bean pot above.

Guernsey Cooking Ware. Back: chocolate cup, 3.75" h., $8-12; shaving mug, 3.25" h., $12-16. Front: custards ranging in height from 3" to 1.5", $4-6 ea.

Guernsey Cooking Ware. Matchholder, $25-30; spice box, $30-35; mustard insert, $8-10; small bowl, $6-8; serving bowl, $14-16; custard, $6-8; individual creamer, $4-6; tumbler, $10-14; creamer (missing lid), $12-14.

Backstamp on bottom of tumbler at left.

Guernsey Cooking Ware. Back: three creamers, one with lid. 4.25" h., $8-12; 5.5" h., $14-18; 3.5" h., $6-10. Front: individual casserole, 4.25" dia., $14-16; condiment jar, 3.25" h., $14-18.

Set of Guernsey Ware covered canisters in graduated sizes: 8" h., $28-34; 6.5" h., $26-32; 4" h., $18-20; cruet, 9" h., $18-22; hanging salt box, 4.5" h., $35-40. All were lettered by hand but have differences in script style.

Guernsey Cooking Ware. Back: ramekin, 6.5" dia., $8-10; individual tea, 4.5" h., $14-16. Front: small bowl, 4.5" dia., $4-6; two condiments (missing lids), $12-14 and $6-8; custard before glazing, $4-6.

Another set of Guernsey Ware covered canisters, ranging in size from 7.5" h., $26-32, to 4" h., $18-20. Shown with hanging salt box, 4.25" h., $35-40.

Trio of Guernsey Cooking Ware items. Cruet, 9" h., $18-22; small covered canister, 4" h., $18-20; small pitcher, 4.25" h., $6-10.

Two Guernsey Ware casseroles with lids, one with fitted silver holder. Left: 5.25" h. x 7.5" dia., $18-22. Right: 5.25" h. x 8.25" dia., $24-28.

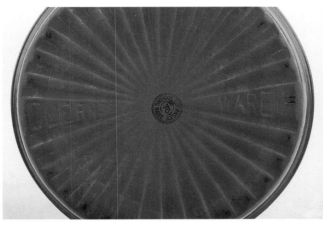

Guernsey Cooking Ware. Pie plate, 10.5" dia., $22-24; smaller pie plate, 8.5" dia., $20-22; mug, 5.25" h., $24-26; milk pitcher, 6.5" h., $26-30.

Backstamp on bottom of smaller pie plate.

Casserole with painted lid and fitted silver holder, Guernsey Cooking Ware. 5.25" h. x 8" dia. $26-30.

Guernsey Cooking Ware. Chocolate pot, 7" h., $20-24; covered oval casserole, 3.25" h., $26-30; individual teapot, 5" h., $12-14.

Guernsey Cooking Ware. Crock, 10"
h., $22-24; covered casserole, 4" h. x
8.5" dia., $22-24; serving bowl, 3" h.
x 9" dia., $12-14.

Individual teapot, Guernsey Ware. 4" h. $14-16.

Backstamp, Guernsey Cooking Ware "Regal-
Rochester."

Backstamp, Guernsey Cooking
Ware, "Hand Painted."

Backstamp from sugar bowl made by
Guernseyware China Company, "G.C.Co.,
Cambridge, China."

Covered casserole with underplate, Guernsey Ware. 4" h. x 8.25" dia. $38-42.

Four cup teapot, Guernsey Ware. 6" h. $28-30.

Guernsey Cooking Ware. Back: covered bowl, 3.25" h. x 5" dia., $12-14. Front: custard cup, 3" h. x 4" dia., $6-8; salt and pepper shakers, 4.5" h., $10-14.

Edgewood style gravy boat, Oxford Potteries line of dinnerware. This is a little known dinnerware line within a company that produced primarily kitchen ware. 8" l. $10-12.

Backstamp, reverse of Edgewood gravy boat.

Two footed bowls, Guernsey Ware, Hotel. Large: 3" h. x 7.25" dia., $12-14; Small: 2.5" h. x 6.5" dia., $10-12.

Guernsey Ware, Hotel. Plate, 8" dia., $6-8; condiment jar, 2.5" h., $4-6.

Two Guernsey Ware, Hotel pieces. Individual creamer, 2.5" h., $4-6; condiment jar, 2.5" h., $12-16.

Guernsey Ware, Hotel. Plate, 8" dia., $6-8; plate, bread and butter, 6.75" dia., $2-3; bowl with bas relief faces on sides, 3" h. x 4.25" dia., $6-8.

Guernsey Ware, Hotel. Small platter, 10" l., $10-12; platter, 11.75" l., $12-14; mug, 3.5" h., $8-12.

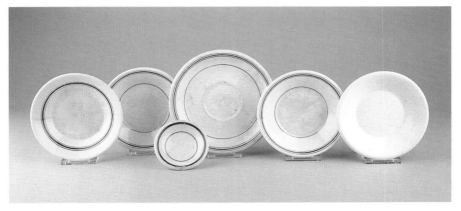

Guernsey Ware, Hotel. Small dishes, 5.25" dia. ea; saucer, 6.25" dia.; butter pat, 3" dia. $2-4 ea.

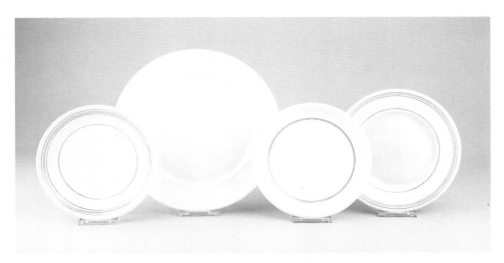

Backstamp, Guernsey Ware, Hotel.

More Guernsey Ware, Hotel pieces. Saucer, 6.25" dia., $2-4; plate, 9" dia., $6-8; saucer, 6.25" dia., $2-4; plate, bread and butter, 6.75" dia., $2-4.

Detail of bas relief faces on the sides of the sugar bowl.

Two pieces of Hotel Ware made by the Guernsey Ware China Company. Sugar bowl with bas relief faces on sides, 4" h., $12-14; small dish, 5" l., $8-10.

Oxford Pottery Co.

On December 23, 1913, a meeting was held in the office of attorney Milton H. Turner to promote this new venture in Cambridge. A site between Burgess and Marquand avenues was purchased, featuring 1.35 acres in Cambridge Township and lots # 54, 55, 56 in the Woodlawn Addition for $1,300.

Articles of incorporation were applied for, and received on December 26, 1913. On February 2, 1914, the new board of directors was: Harry W. Dennis, president; William Rigby, vice-president; U.G. Henderson, secretary; and T.M. Bond, treasurer.

Charles E. Maier and his brother Lewis E. Maier came from a pottery at Paden City, West Virginia, to supervise the work at the Oxford Pottery Company. On August 12, 1914, Thomas H. Snyder resigned as superintendent of the Paden City Pottery to become superintendent of the Oxford Pottery Company; production began in September of that same year.

On November 28, 1914 an advertisement in the *Guernsey Times* noted that the Oxford Pottery Company plant comprised more than two-thirds of an acre in floor space and boasted the slogan "One hour's experience with 'Oxfordware' means a Life-long Friendship."

On August 1, 1916, Charles E. Maier was granted a patent by the U.S. Patent Office on the Oxford Odorless Water Seal; the brown with white lined vessel is hermetically sealed and uses only a small amount of water for cooking.

In 1934, the Oxford Pottery Company assets were absorbed by the Universal Potteries, Inc.

Photograph showing employees of the Oxford Pottery Co., c. 1920s.

Four cup teapot, 6" h., $16-22; butter, 1 lb., 3.25" h. x 5.75" l., $26-32; creamer, 4.5" h., $12-14; water jug, 8.5" h., $27-30; water jug, 7.5" h., $35-40.

Three refrigerator bowls, missing lids. 4.25" h. x 6" dia., $12-14; 3.5" h. x 5.25" dia., $8-12; 2.5" h. x 4.25" dia., $6-10.

Shaker, 4.75" h., $8-12; bean pot, 3" h., $6-8; refrigerator bowl, 2.5" h., $6-8.

Four cup teapot, 6" h., $28-30; mug, 4.5" h., $16-20.

Back: pitcher, 4.5" h., $15-20; decorated pitcher, 4.75" h., $18-22. Front: bean pot, 2.75" h., $6-8; mug, 4.5" h., $16-20.

Back: water jug with ice lip, 7" h., $30-35; mug, 4.5" h., $16-20; two cup teapot, 5.5" h., $22-26. Front: French casserole, 3.5" h. x 5" dia., $12-14; small bowl, 2.5" h. x 5" dia., $8-12; one cup teapot, known as a "Pix," 4.5" h., $12-14.

Snowdrop design assortment. Back: water jug with lid, 9.25" h., $28-32; milk pitcher, 6" h., $18-22; mug, 4.5" h., $16-20. Front: covered bowl, 4.25" dia., $12-14; refrigerator bowl, 3" h. x 4" dia., $8-10; bean pot, 2.75" h. x 3" dia., $6-8; custard, 2.5" h. x 3.25" dia., $4-6. The Snowdrop design was created by Howard B. Potts.

Two cup teapot, 5.25" h., $22-26; bowl, 2.5" h. x 5" dia., $12-14; water jug, 7.5" h., $35-40; mug, 4.5" h., $16-20.

Right:
Cookie jar, missing lid. 9" h. $38-40.

Four cup teapot in Snowdrop design, marked "1943 Cambridge, Ohio" on one side and "Mr. and Mrs. W.R. Palmer" on other. Signed by "Roy M. Potts, Byesville, OH," the brother of Howard B. Potts. Note that the Oxfordware line was carried on by Universal after it took over the Oxford Pottery Co., accounting for the date of 1943 on this teapot. $28-30.

Back: large mixing bowl, Mount Vernon shape, 4" h. x 10.5" dia., $20-24; teapot, 5.5" h., $35-40. Front: creamer, 4.25" h., $12-14; small mixing bowl, 3" h. x 6" dia., $8-12; bean pot, 3" h., $6-8.

Creamer, 4.25" h., $12-14; bowl, 2.5" h. x 5.25" dia., $12-14; bean pot, 3" h., $6-8; shaker, 4.5" h., $6-8.

Two pitchers, not the regular line of colors. These may have been experimental or special order colors. 4.75" h., $18-22 ea. Custard cup, 2.5" h. x 3.25" dia., $4-6.

Teapot, 7" h., $16-20; teapot, 5.5" h., $12-14; bowl, 3" h. x 6" dia., $12-14; ramekin, 1.5" h. x 7" l., $8-12.

Backstamp, reverse of one of the pieces in the photo above.

Bowl, 2.5" h. x 5" dia., $6-10; covered refrigerator bowl, 4" h. x 5" dia., $14-16.

Below:
Bean pot, 3" h., $6-8; covered casserole, 5" h. x 8.5" dia., $28-30; covered refrigerator bowl, 3" h. x 4.25" dia., $10-12.

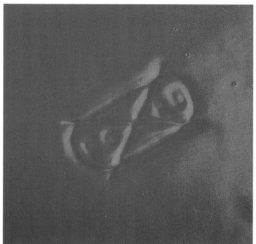

Backstamp, reverse of covered casserole at left.

Large mixing bowl, 4.75" h. x 9.25" dia., $18-20; small mixing bowl, 3" h. x 6.25" dia., $8-12; teapot, 6" h., $28-30.

Universal salad fork and spoon, originally made by Oxford and carried over to the Universal years. $18-22 pr.

The Atlas-Globe China Co.

On Monday, June 8, 1925, the Globe China Company, successors of the Guernseyware Company, began production. The Atlas China Company, located about one hundred miles north of Cambridge in Niles, Ohio, was the parent company. The new company had two hundred employees under the organization of Mr. George Ahrendts of Niles, along with a Mr. Stevens and Mr. Gilmor. Mr. Ahrendts was general manager and W.E. Tritt was factory superintendent. Tableware was manufactured exclusively by Globe in both white and decorated.

In 1926, the Globe China Company consolidated with the Atlas China Company of Niles and Atlas moved their corporate office to Cambridge, Ohio. The Niles plant, which had been destroyed by fire in 1925, was rebuilt and then closed in 1928. The machinery was taken out in 1934 when it was acquired by Universal Potteries, Inc.

The Atlas-Globe trademark was copyrighted in November 1926. Deed records show the purchase of Globe by Atlas on May 27, 1927. By 1933 the combined Atlas-Globe company faced hard times and foreign imports forced the plant to close.

Left:
Two pieces from the Atlas China Company, originally the parent company of Atlas-Globe. Soup tureen, 3" h. x 9" l., $24-28; sugar, 3" h., $12-14.

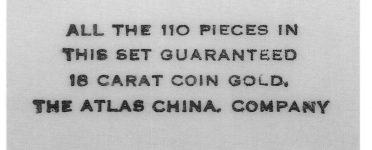

ALL THE 110 PIECES IN THIS SET GUARANTEED 18 CARAT COIN GOLD. THE ATLAS CHINA COMPANY

Backstamp from sugar, The Atlas China Company.

Globe China Company assortment. Cup and saucer, 2.25" h., $8-10; plate, 9 1/8" dia., $6-10.

Globe China Company. Sugar, 3" h., $12-14; soup tureen, 3" h. x 9" l., $24-28; gravy boat, 8" l., $14-16.

Gravy boat, Globe China Company. 7.25" l. $14-16.

Globe China Company. Saucer, 5.75" dia., $2-4; sugar, 3.25" h., $12-14; soup tureen, 3" h. x 9" l., $24-28; teacup, 2.25" h., $4-6; two plates, bread and butter, 6" dia., $2-3 ea.

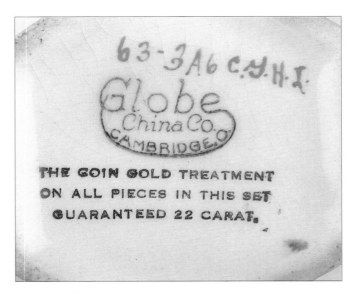

Backstamp from creamer.

Two pieces from the Globe China Company. Gravy boat, 7.5" l., $14-16; creamer, 2.75" l., $10-12.

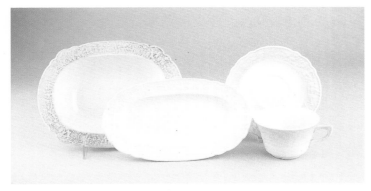

Old Holland Ware, made by the Atlas-Globe China Co. Vegetable dish, 2" h. x 9.25" l., $8-12; pickle dish, 9" l., $8-12; cup and saucer, 2.5" h., $8-10. Old Holland gets its name from the raised figures on the plate shoulder depicting a Dutch scene. Later, during the Universal Pottery years, it was known as Netherlands.

Old Holland Ware. Bowl, 5.75" dia., $4-6; plate, bread and butter, 6.25" dia., $2-3; bowl, 5.75" dia., $4-6.

Decorative/commemorative plates in two sizes, Old Holland Ware. 10" sq., $15-20; 6.25" sq., $12-16 ea.

Two pieces of Old Holland Ware. Sugar, 4.5" h., $10-12; bouillon, 2.5" h., $12-14.

Gravy boat, Old Holland Ware. 3.25" h. $12-14.

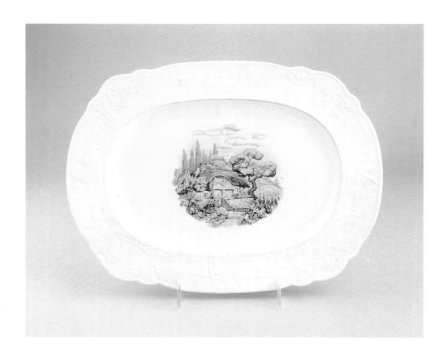

Platter, Old Holland Ware. 9" h. x
11.75" l., $12-14.

Two plates, Old Holland Ware. 9"
dia. $6-8 ea.

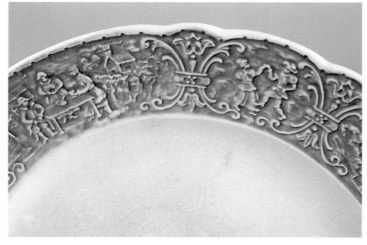

Detail of pattern on Old Holland Ware plate with blue border.

Plates, Old Holland Ware. 9.25" dia. $6-8 ea.

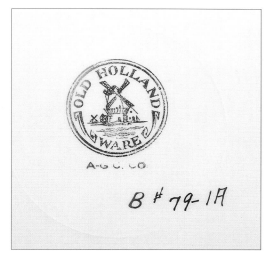

Plates, Old Holland Ware. 9" dia. $6-8 ea.

Backstamp, Old Holland Ware.

Royal soup with underplate, Cambridge Ivory shape, made by the Atlas-Globe China Company. Bowl: 5" dia.; underplate, 6.75" dia. $14-18 set.

Two pieces in Cambridge Ivory shape, made by the Atlas-Globe China Company. Gravy boat, 8" l., $14-16; platter, 9.5" dia., $14-16.

Sugar and creamer with different decorations, Cambridge Ivory shape, made by the Atlas-Globe China Company. Sugar: 3.25" h., $12-14; creamer: 3" h., $10-12.

Cambridge Ivory shape, made by Atlas-Globe China Company. Vegetable dish, 2.5" h. x 8.75" dia., $8-12; creamer, 3" h., $8-10.

Two saucers, Cambridge Ivory shape, made by Atlas-Globe China Company. 5.75" dia. $2-4 ea.

Backstamp, Cambridge Ivory, A.G.C.Co.

Plate, bread and butter, Cambridge Ivory shape, made by Atlas-Globe China Company. 6" dia. $4-6.

Backstamp, Cambridge Ivory, A.G.C.Co.

Three vegetable dishes in Oxford Ivory, made by the Atlas-Globe China Company. 9.25" dia., $8-12; 8.75" dia., $6-10; 9 1/8" l., $8-10.

Oxford Ivory. Teacup, 2.25" h., $2-4; plate, 8.5" dia., $6-8; plate, bread and butter, 6" dia., $2-3.

Two platters, Oxford Ivory. Large: 13.25" l., $14-16; Small: 11.75" l., $12-14.

Backstamp, Oxford Ivory.

Oxford Ivory. Soup tureen, 3" h. x 10.25" l., $35-40; creamer, 3.5" h., $8-10.

Backstamp, Oxford Ivory.

Creamer, Atlas-Globe China Company. 2.75" h.. $12-14.

Royal soup, Atlas-Globe China Company. 5 1/8" dia. $10-12.

Teacup, Atlas-Globe China Company. 2" h.. $2-4.

Backstamp from bottom of royal soup above.

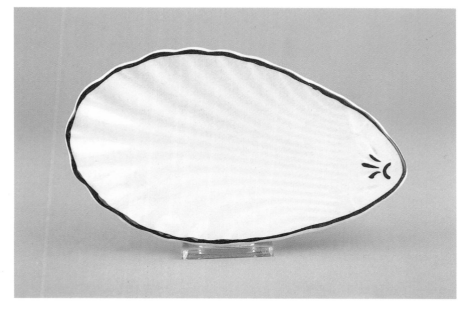

Soap dish, Atlas-Globe China Company. 7.5" l.. $12-14.

Two pieces from the Atlas-Globe China Company. Sugar/footed bowl, 3" h., $12-14; creamer, 3.5" h., $10-12.

Atlas-Globe China Company. Creamer, 3" h., $8-10; platter, 10" h. x 13.5" l., $14-16; plate, 9" dia., $6-8.

Atlas-Globe China Company. Plate, salad, 7" dia., $3-4; cup, 2.25" h., $4-5; vegetable dish, 2.5" h. x 8.5" dia., $8-10.

Broadway Rose shape, made by Atlas-Globe China Co. Gravy boat, 9" l., $14-16; plate, 9" dia., $6-8; cup, 2.5" h., $8-12; oval vegetable bowl, 2" h. x 9" l., $10-14.

Broadway Rose shape, made by Atlas-Globe China Co. Plate, square salad, 6.25" sq., $4-6; cup, 2.5" h., $8-12; oval platter, 11.5" l., $16-18; creamer, 3.25" h., $8-12; fruit, 5.25" dia., $4-6.

Backstamp, Broadway Rose.

Universal Potteries, Inc.

By May 11, 1934, Universal Potteries had incorporated to acquire the Atlas-Globe China Company and Oxford Pottery Company. Employment started at 200, with hopes of reaching 650 employees at full production and shipments annually in excess of 1.5 million dollars. At their annual meeting in 1947, The United States Potters Association reported record sales of dinnerware since World War II and was hoping to increase output in 1948 with further expansion and growth. Also in 1947, Universal Potteries, Inc. built Plant No. 3 with 85,000 square feet on the site of an old tin mill and hired 200 people (Plant No. 1 was referred to as the Guernseyware plant and Plant No. 2, originally completed in 1914, was referred to as the Oxford plant).

Postcard showing aerial view of Universal Potteries' "three modern plants," c. 1940s-50s.

A large block of stock was purchased in 1934 by the McClelland family of Barnesville, Ohio, and they appointed G.D. Agnew as manager.

In 1934, the officers of Universal Potteries, Inc. were: H.D. McClelland, president and chairman of the board; G.D. Agnew, vice president and general manager; Paul T. McClelland, treasurer; John W. Riemenschneider, secretary; F.L. Maris, assistant treasurer; and C. S. Wardeska, assistant secretary.

Photograph from the 69th Annual Dinner of the United States Potter's Association at the Hotel Astor in New York, Dec. 9th, 1947, with G.D. Agnew as retiring President. Agnew was also an officer of Universal Potteries at the time. Also shown are other employees of Universal.

Universal products were semi-porcelain dinnerware and kitchenware and the company was reputed as the originator and leader in production of refrigerator ware. Universal Potteries were noted for their distinctive shapes, such as Camwood Ivory (a combination of the words "Cambridge" and "Edgewood"), Upico (derived from the company's initials and characterized by indented rings around the ware), and Ballerina (a line of multicolored ware designed to compete with Fiesta), as well as Vogue, Fascination, Raymor, Leaf Fantasy, and Oxfordware. Many popular shapes were carried over from the Oxford and Atlas-Globe companies with only the backstamps changing.

A large number of the popular decorations familiar to collectors today can be found on most of Universal's shapes; examples of these decorations are Cattail—the most popular throughout the 1940s and 1950s—Bittersweet, Circus, American Beauty, Roy Rogers, Elsie and her family, Calico Fruit, Bamboo, Butterfly, Southern Gardens, and Magnolia.

Many decals were purchased from the Universal Decal Company of East Liverpool, Ohio, which explains the same decals being used by several potteries. If a special decal was needed—such as the Country Club—it was designed and produced on the grounds.

Arden Kail, who worked in the decorating department as a liner, remembers the Cattail pattern as a very popular line in the 1940s. He states that Mose Aleshire would push carts loaded with hundreds of dozens of pieces to be "red-lined." He added that the liners (people that painted the lines around the edges) were paid three cents per dozen.

By 1957, Universal Potteries, Inc. was phasing out their dinnerware line. They had incorporated a line of tile in 1955, which they called Oxford. On September 1, 1960 the company liquidated their dinnerware division completely and suspended operations of Plants No. 1 and No. 3, using them instead for the storage of ceramic tile accessories.

A year later, Universal Potteries, Inc. was involved in an exchange of stock ownership, with G.D. Agnew, president; Richard M. Mayor, vice-president; C.S. Wardeska, treasurer; and attorney D. Deemor Agnew, secretary. This took place on September 1, 1961.

Camwood Ivory shape. Oval vegetable bowl, 7" h. x 8.75" l., $8-12; sugar (missing lid), 3.75" h., $10-12.

Camwood Ivory shape. Plate, 9" dia., $6-8; fruit, 5.25" dia., $2-4; saucer, 5.75" dia., $2-4.

Mt. Vernon shape. Shaker, 4.5" h., $6-8; pitcher, 5" h., $20-24.

Ballerina shape. Cup and saucer, 2.25" h., $8-10; coupe soup, 7.75" dia., $6-8; fruit, 5.25" dia., $2-4.

Ballerina shape. Oatmeal, 6" dia., $4-6; sugar, 4" h., $10-12.

Camwood Ivory shape. Plate, 9" dia., $6-8; sugar (missing lid), 3.5" h., $10-12; creamer, 3.5" h., $8-10.

Backstamp, Sheffield.

Sheffield shape. Plate, 8.25" dia., $6-8; cup, 2.25" h., $2-4.

Sweet William decoration on Camwood Ivory shape. Platter, 11.5" dia., $14-16; cup, 2.25" h., $2-4.

Old Curiosity Shop decoration on Camwood Ivory shape. Cup and saucer, 2.25" h., $8-10; oval platter, 6" h. x 12.75" l., $14-16; plate, bread and butter, 6.25" dia., $3-4.

Old Curiosity Shop decoration on Camwood Ivory shape. Plate, 9.75" dia., $6-8; coupe soup, 7.75" dia., $6-8.

Old Curiosity Shop decoration on Camwood Ivory shape. Oval vegetable bowl, 7" h. x 9" l., $8-12; pitcher, 7" h., $6-8.

Backstamp, Old Curiosity Shop decoration.

Camwood Ivory shape. Teacup, 2.25" h., $2-4; plate, 9" dia., $6-8; sugar, $10-12; and creamer, $8-10, 3.5" h. each.

Camwood Ivory shape. Creamer, 3.5" h., $8-10; plate, 10" dia., $6-10; plate, bread and butter, 6" dia., $2-3.

Camwood Ivory shape. Batter tray, 11.5" dia., $18-22; milk pitcher, 6" h., $16-20.

Camwood Ivory shape. Cup and saucer, 2.5" h., $8-10; platter, 11.5" dia., $14-16; plate, 9" dia., $6-8; plate, bread and butter, 6.25" dia., $2-3.

Camwood Ivory shape. Nappy, 9.5" dia., $8-12; nappy, 8.75" dia., $8-10; oval vegetable bowl, 7" h. x 9" l., $8-12.

Camwood Ivory shape. Covered casserole, 3.5" h., $24-30; sugar, 4" h., $10-12; creamer, 3.5" h., $8-10.

Camwood Ivory shape. Platter, 11.5" dia., $14-16; fruit, 5.25" dia., $2-4; coupe soup, 7.75" dia., $6-8.

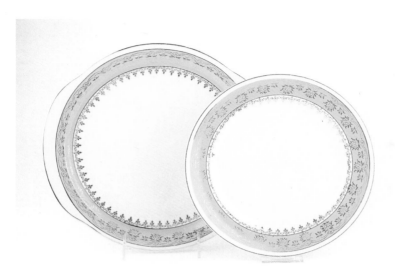

Camwood Ivory shape. Platter, 10.75" dia., $12-14; plate, 9 1/8" dia., $6-8.

Camwood Ivory shape. Platter, 10.75" dia., $12-14; saucer, 5.75" dia., $2-4.

Camwood Ivory shape. Back: plate, 9.75" dia., $6-8; coupe soup, 7.75" dia., $6-8; grill plate, 9.75" dia., $10-14. Front: bowl, 3" h. x 5.5" dia., $10-14; cream soup lug, 6.5" dia., $10-14; sugar, 4.5" h., $10-12.

Camwood Ivory shape. Nappy, 2.75" h. x 8.75" dia., $10-14; platter, 13.5" dia., $14-16; salt and pepper shakers, 3.75" h., $8-12; gravy boat, 8" l., $12-14.

Assortment in Cherrytone decoration. Shaker, Upico shape, 4.25" h., $10-12; ice lip pitcher, Ballerina shape, 7.5" h., $30-35; salt and pepper shakers, Vogue shape, 3" h., $8-12; sugar, Camwood Ivory shape with Indian Tree design, 4" h., $14-16.

Cherrytone decoration on Camwood Ivory shape. Four cup teapot, 6" h., $27-32; salt and pepper shakers, 3.5" h., $8-12; water jug with damaged lid, 6.75" h., $35-40; custard cup, 2.75" h. x 3.25" dia., $4-6; water jug with ice lip, 7.25" h., $35-40.

Cherrytone decoration on Camwood Ivory shape. Lidded pitcher, 5.75" h., $18-22; salt and pepper shakers, 4" h., $8-12; plate, 10" dia., $6-10; plate, 9" dia., $6-8; saucer, 5.75" dia., $2-4; cup, 2.5" h., $6-8.

Cherrytone decoration on Ballerina shape, Kitchenware line. Back: 6 cup teapot, 5" h., $30-32; salad bowl, 9" dia., $16-20. Front: covered casserole, 4" h. x 8.5" dia., on plate, 10" dia., $28-32; salt and pepper shakers, 4" h., $8-12; covered refrigerator bowl, 4" h. x 5" dia., $12-14; 3 piece bowl set, 6.5", 7.5", and 8.5" dia., $20-24.

Assortment in Cherrytone decoration. Back: large covered refrigerator bowl, 4.5" h. x 6" dia., $14-16; covered casserole in Camwood Ivory shape, 3.75" h. x 8" dia., $28-30; medium covered refrigerator bowl, 3.75" h. x 5" dia., $12-14; sugar and creamer, 3.25" h., $12-16; one cup teapot, 4.5" h., $12-14; small refrigerator bowl, 2.75" h. x 4" dia., $4-6.

More Cherrytone pieces. Covered bowl, 2.5" h. x 5" dia., $12-14; mixing bowl, 3.5" h. x 10" dia., $16-20; pitcher, 6" h., $15-20; salt and pepper shakers, 4" h., $8-12; French casserole, 2.25" h. x 5" dia., $12-14; fork and spoon, $22-28.

Newspaper advertisement for 12-piece Cherrytone set sold at Davis Department Store, Cambridge, Ohio.

43

Camwood Ivory shape. Plate, 9.75" dia., $8-10; plate, bread and butter, 5.75" dia., $2-3; vegetable dish, 2" h. x 9" dia., $8-12; creamer, 3.5" h., $8-10.

Water jug, Universal, 6.75" h., $35-40; Cup, Ballerina shape, 2.25" h., $2-4; Cup, Camwood Ivory shape, 2.75" h., $2-4.

Detail of windmill design.

Calico Fruit decoration on Camwood Ivory shape. Water jug with lid, 6" h., $40-55; shaker, 3.75" h., $8-12; lidded pitcher, 7.5" h., 40-45; one cup teapot, 4.75" h., 25-27.

Calico Fruit decoration on Camwood Ivory shape. Salad bowl, 3.5" h. x 9.75" dia., $18-22; small bowl, 3" h. x 6" dia., $10-14; casserole (missing lid), 3.5" h. x 8.25" dia., $18-22; grill plate, 9.5" dia., $12-14; cover for refrigerator bowl, 5" dia., $4-6.

Backstamp, Calico Fruit decoration.

Circus decoration on Camwood Ivory shape. Coupe soup, 7.75" dia., $4-6; underplate from batter set, 11" dia., $14-16; bread and butter plate, 6" dia., $2-3; plate, 9" dia., $8-10; sugar, 4" h., $10-12; teapot, 4.5" h., $14-16.

Circus decoration on Upico shape. Covered casserole, 3.5" h. x 8.25" dia., $24-28; water jug, 9" h., $38-40; plate, 9.25" dia., $8-10; milk pitcher, 6.75" dia., $22-26.

Camwood Ivory shape. Beverage set with six tumblers and metal clip-on handle. Server: 10" dia., $10-12. Tumblers: 3" h., $6-8 ea.

Pitcher, Camwood Ivory, part of the beverage set shown above. 7.75" h. $35-40.

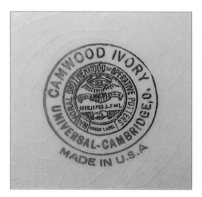

Backstamp, Camwood Ivory.

46

Poppy decoration on Camwood Ivory shape. Platter, 10.25" h. x 13.5" l., $14-16; plate, 9 1/8" dia., $6-8; creamer, 3.5" h., $8-10.

Poppy decoration on Camwood Ivory. Platter, 10.75" dia., $14-16; grill plate, 9.75" dia., $10-14.

Poppy decoration on Mount Vernon shape. Plate, 7" dia., $4-6; individual casserole, 6" dia., $4-6; plate, square salad, 7.25" sq., $6-8.

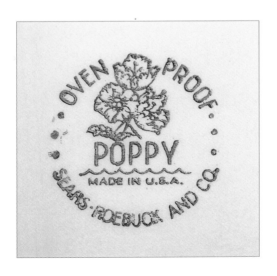

Left:
Backstamp, Poppy decoration. Sears Roebuck and Co. contracted with Universal Potteries to make several lines of dinnerware so that they could sell it in their well-known catalog.

Backstamp, Mount Vernon shape.

Hollyhock decoration on Camwood Ivory shape. Plate, bread and butter, 6" dia., $2-3; saucer, 5.75" dia., $2-3; gravy boat, 8" l., $12-14.

Covered bean pot. Hollyhock decoration on Camwood Ivory shape. 5.75" h. $18-22.

Hollyhock decoration on two different shapes. Vegetable dish, Camwood Ivory shape, 2" h. x 9" l., $8-12; plate, Mount Vernon shape, 9" sq., $6-8.

Camwood Ivory shape (with gold trim). Refrigerator container with lid, 3.75" h. x 8" l., $18-24; refrigerator container without lid, 2.75" h. x 9.5" l., $16-22.

Camwood Ivory shape (with gold trim). Plate, bread and butter, 6.25" dia., $2-3; saucer, 5.75" dia., $2-3; coupe soup, 7.75" dia., $4-6; fruit, 5.25" dia., $2-4; sugar, 3.5" h., $10-12.

Cup and saucer, Camwood Ivory shape, $8-10.

Camwood Ivory shape. Sugar, 3.25" h., $10-12; creamer, 3.25" h., $8-10; plate, 10" dia., $6-10; plate, salad, 7" dia., $3-4; cup and saucer, 2.25" h., $8-10.

Camwood Ivory shape. Coupe soup, 7.75" dia., $6-8; large vegetable dish, 2.75" h. x 9.5" dia., $8-12; vegetable dish, 2.5" h. x 8.5" dia., $8-10; gravy boat, 8" l., $12-14.

Camwood Ivory shape. Vegetable dish, 2" h. x 9" l., $8-12; large platter, 10" h. x 13.5" l., $14-16; platter, 9" h. x 11.5" l., $12-14.

Camwood Ivory shape. Covered casserole, wide lip, 2.25" h. x 9.5" dia., $24-30; platter, 10" h. x 11.5" l., $14-16.

Camwood Ivory shape. Cup and saucer, 2.5" h., $8-10; sugar, 3.5" h., $10-12; creamer, 3.5" h., $8-10.

Camwood Ivory shape. Fruit, 5.25" dia., $2-4; bowl, 3" h., 5.25" dia., $6-8; butter, 1/4 lb., $14-16; salt and pepper shakers, 4.25" h., $8-12.

Camwood Ivory shape. Vegetable dish, 2.5" h. x 8.75" dia., $8-12; coupe soup, 7.75" dia., $4-6; plate, salad, 7.25" dia., $3-4; plate, bread and butter, 6" dia., $2-3.

Camwood Ivory shape. Plate, 9" dia., $6-8; platter, 9.5" dia., $8-12; vegetable dish, 2" h. x 9" l., $8-12.

Covered casserole, handled, Camwood Ivory. 3.5" h. x 7.5" dia. $24-30.

Camwood Ivory shape. Covered casserole, 2.5" h. x 6.5" dia., $12-14; plate, bread and butter, 6.25" dia., $2-3; saucer, 5.75" dia., $2-4; cup, 2.5" h., $2-4.

Camwood Ivory shape. Plate, 9" dia., $6-8; creamer, 3.5" h., $8-10.

Camwood Ivory shape. Platter, 11" h. x 13.25" l., $12-14; pickle, 9.25" l., $9-12.

Cup and saucer, Camwood Ivory. 2.25" h. $8-10.

Covered casserole, Mount Vernon. 4" h. $28-30.

Assortment of pieces with gold trim and Universal backstamp. Bowl, 3.5" h. x 6" dia., $6-8; salt and pepper shakers, 4" h., $8-12; milk pitcher, 6" h., $20-22.

Rambler Rose decoration on Camwood Ivory shape. Gravy boat, 8" l., $12-14; water jug with ice lip, 6" h., $35-40; creamer, 3.5" h., $8-10.

Rambler Rose decoration on Camwood Ivory shape. Teacup, 2.25" h., $2-4; vegetable dish, 2.75" h. x 9.5" dia., $8-12; sugar, 3.25" h., $10-12.

Rambler Rose decoration on Camwood Ivory shape. Water jug, 7.25" h., $35-40; plate, 10" dia., $6-10; lid, 5.5" dia., $4-8.

Rambler Rose decoration on Camwood Ivory shape. Coupe soup, 7.75" dia., $4-6; platter, 10.5" h. x 13.5" l., $12-14; salt and pepper shakers, 4" h., $8-12.

Camwood Ivory shape (with gold trim). Oval vegetable bowl, 2" h. x 9" l., $8-12; platter, 11.5" dia., $12-14; oatmeal, 6" dia., $2-4.

Camwood Ivory shape (with gold trim). Plate, 9" dia., $6-8; saucer, 5.75" dia., $2-4; plate, bread and butter, 6.25" dia., $2-3.

Camwood Ivory (with gold trim). Vegetable dish, 2.5" h. x 8.75" dia., $8-10; creamer, 3.5" h., $8-10; sugar, 3.5" h., $10-12.

Camwood Ivory shape. Teacup, 2.5" h., $2-4; plate, 9" dia., $6-8; saucer, 5.75" dia., $2-4; plate, bread and butter, 6" dia., $2-3.

Camwood Ivory shape. Grill plate, 9.75" dia., $10-14; fruit, 5" dia., $2-4.

Desert Cactus decoration on Camwood Ivory shape (with gold trim). Refrigerator bowl, 4.75" h. x 6" dia., $12-14; salt and pepper shakers, 3.75" h., $8-12.

Camwood Ivory shape. Coupe soup, 7.75" dia., $4-6; plate, 9.75" dia., $6-8, saucer, 5.75" dia., $2-4; teacup, 2.25" h., $2-4.

Camwood Ivory shape. Sugar, 3.5" h., $10-12; creamer, 3.5" h., $8-10; plate, bread and butter, 6" dia., $2-4.

Camwood Ivory shape. Platter, 10.25" h. x 13.5" l., $14-16; fruit, 5.25" dia., $2-4; vegetable dish, 2.5" h. x 8.75" dia., $8-12.

Cattail decoration on Camwood Ivory shape. Small covered refrigerator bowl, 3" h., $10-12; plate, 9 1/8" dia., $8-14; plate, salad, 7.25" dia., $3-4; saucer, 5.75" dia., $3-5; teacup, 2.5" h., $3-5.

Cattail decoration on Camwood Ivory shape (with red trim). Plate, 9.75" dia., $8-14; cup, 2.5" h., $3-5; saucer, 5.75" dia., $3-5.

Cattail decoration on Old Holland shape. Saucer, 6" dia., $3-5; plate, 9 1/8" dia., $8-14; teacup, 2.5" h., $3-5.

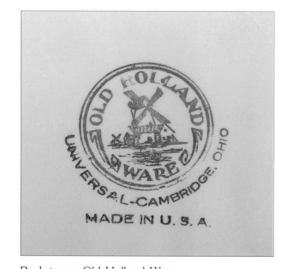

Backstamp, Old Holland Ware.

Cattail decoration on Ballerina shape. Casserole lid, 8.25" dia., $6-8; teacup, 2.25" h., $3-5.

Cattail decoration on Upico shape. Covered refrigerator bowl, 3" h. x 5.5" dia., $18-20; shaker, 4.25" h., $10-12.

Cattail decoration on Camwood Ivory shape. Vegetable dish, 2.5" h. x 8.75" dia., $8-10; large vegetable dish, 3" h. x 9.75" dia., $8-12; coupe soup, 7.75" dia., $6-8.

Cattail decoration. Water jug, 6.5" h., $35-40; cracker jar, 7" h., $30-35; water jug, 6" h., $40-45.

Cookie jar, Cattail decoration. 8.25" h. $100-120.

Covered refrigerator bowl, Cattail decoration.
3.5" h. x 7" dia., $20-24.

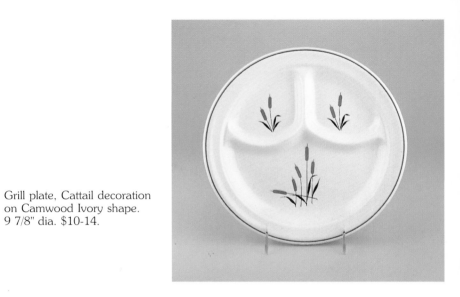

Grill plate, Cattail decoration
on Camwood Ivory shape.
9 7/8" dia. $10-14.

Three covered casseroles in Cattail decoration, various shapes. From left: 3.5" h. x 8.25" dia., $22-26; 3.75" h. x 8.25" dia., $22-26; 3.75" h. x 8.5" dia., $30-35.

Set of three nesting bowls, Cattail decoration on Camwood
Ivory shape. 5", 3.75", and 3" h. $42-48 set.

Saucer, Cattail decoration on Camwood Ivory shape (with platinum banding), 5.75" dia., $4-6; saucer, Cattail decoration on Laurella shape, 6" dia., $4-6.

Cattail decoration on Camwood Ivory shape (with gold trim). Gravy boat, 8" l., $12-14; sugar, 3.5" h., $10-12; creamer, 3.5" h., $8-10.

Cattail decoration on Mount Vernon shape. Salt and pepper shakers, 4.25" h., $10-14; set of three nesting bowls, 4.5", 3.75", and 2.75" h., $44-50; custard cup, 2.5" h., $4-6.

Cattail decoration on Mount Vernon shape. Plate, bread and butter, 6" dia., $4-6; cup and saucer, 2.25" h., $8-14; milk pitcher, 6.75" h., $40-45; teapot, 5.5" h., $40-45.

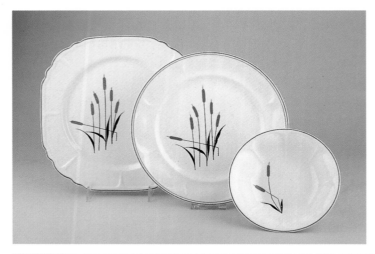

Cattail decoration on Mount Vernon shape.
Plate, 9.75" sq., $8-14; plate, 9" dia., $8-12;
oatmeal, 5.75" dia., $6-8.

Cattail decoration on Mount Vernon shape.
Platter, 11.5" l., $14-16; vegetable dish, 3.25"
x 7 3/8" dia., $12-14.

Backstamp, Mount Vernon shape.

Cattail decoration. Salt and pepper shakers, Camwood Ivory shape, 4" h., $10-14; platter,
Camwood Ivory shape, 11.25" l., $12-14; tumbler, Camwood Ivory shape, 4.5" h., $20-24;
water jug with ice lip, 5.5" h., $35-40.

Cattail decoration. Large platter, Camwood Ivory shape, 14.5" l., $14-16; pickle, Camwood Ivory shape, 9.25" l., $8-12; platter, Camwood Ivory shape, 11.5" l., $12-14; creamer, $8-10; and sugar, $10-12, Camwood Ivory shape, 3.5" h.; milk jug, 6" h., $20-22.

Cattail decoration on Camwood Ivory shape. Cream soup, lug, 5 7/8" dia., $6-8; large platter, 10.75" dia., $12-14; salt and pepper shakers, 4.25" h., $12-16; platter, 9.5" dia., $12-14; plate, square salad, 7.25" sq., $6-8; fruit, 5.25" dia., $2-4.

Cattail decoration on Camwood Ivory shape. Gravy boat, 8" dia., $12-14; platter, 11.25" l., $12-14; plate, bread and butter, 6" dia., $2-3; pie plate, 10" dia., $16-22; custard cup, 2.5" h., $4-6; covered bowl, 2.5" h. x 5" dia., $10-14.

Cattail decoration. Butter, 1 lb., $35-40; batter tray, 11.5" dia., $18-22; bean pot, 5.5" h., $18-24; water jug, 6" h., $35-40; server, 9" l., $14-18.

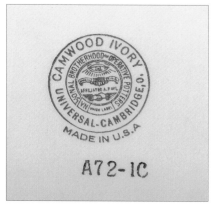

Backstamp, Camwood Ivory Cattail. Not all backstamps for Cattail included the name, but each specific piece had a number by which it was known.

Backstamp, Camwood Ivory Cattail decoration.

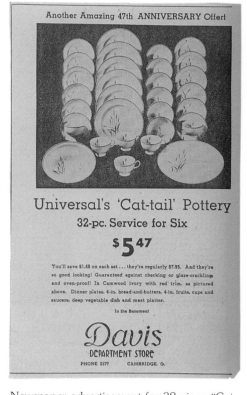
Newspaper advertisement for 32-piece "Cattail" set sold at Davis Department Store, Cambridge, Ohio.

62

Camwood Ivory shape. Bean pot, 2.75" h., $6-8; plate, 9" dia., $6-10; sugar, 3.5" h., $10-12; creamer, 3.5" h., $8-10.

Garden Glory decoration on Camwood Ivory shape. Covered refrigerator bowl, 4.75" h. x 6" dia., $12-14; teacup, 2.5" h., $2-4.

Garden Glory decoration on Camwood Ivory shape. Plate, bread and butter, 6.25" dia., $2-4; plate, 9.75" dia., $6-8; plate, 9" dia., $6-8; cream soup, lug, 6" dia., $6-8.

Platter, Cottage Garden decoration on Camwood Ivory shape. 12.75" l.. $12-14.

Two pieces in Cottage Garden decoration. Cracker jar, Universal, 7" h., $30-35; tumbler, 4.5" h., $10-14.

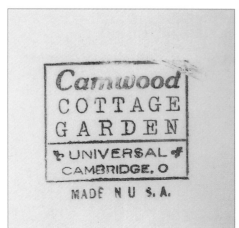

Backstamp, Camwood Cottage Garden.

American Beauty Rose
decoration on
Camwood Ivory.
Teacup, 2.5" h., $2-4;
plate, 10" dia., $6-10;
French casserole, 2.25"
h. x 5" dia., $12-14;
footed bowl, 3" h. x
5.25" dia., $6-8.

American Beauty Rose decoration on
Camwood Ivory shape. Salad bowl, 3.5" h.
x 10" dia., $16-18; water jug with ice lip,
6.25" h., $35-40.

Backstamp, American Beauty
Rose decoration.

Camwood Ivory shape, various decorations. Two creamers, 3.5" h., $8-10 ea.; gravy boat, 8" l., $12-14.

Camwood Ivory shape, various decorations. Saucer, 5.75" dia., $2-3; two plates, bread and butter, 6" dia., $3-4 ea.

Camwood Ivory shape, various decorations. From left: Plate, bread and butter, 6" dia., $2-3; plate, salad, 7.25" dia., $3-4; plate, bread and butter, 6" dia., $2-3; plate, bread and butter, 6" dia., $2-3; saucer, 5.75" dia., $2-3.

Camwood Ivory shape, various decorations. Platter, 11.5" l., $8-12; plate, 9" dia., $6-8.

Camwood Ivory, various decorations. French casserole, 2.25" h. x 5" dia., $12-14; platter, 13.25" l., $14-16.

Mount Vernon shape. Plate, 9" dia., $6-8; saucer, 5.75" dia., $2-4.

Camwood Ivory, various decorations. Plates, 9" dia. $6-8 ea.

Covered refrigerator bowl, Mount Vernon shape. 3" h. x 6.25" dia. $12-16.

Camwood Ivory shape. Saucer, 5.75" dia., $2-4; plate, 9 1/8" dia., $6-8; plate, bread and butter, 6" dia., $2-3; fruit, 5.25" dia., $2-4.

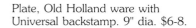

Plate, Old Holland ware with Universal backstamp. 9" dia. $6-8.

Milk pitcher, Mount Vernon shape with Universal backstamp, 5" h., $20-22; water jug, Universal, 6.5" h., $35-40; bean pot, Universal, 5.75" h., $18-22.

Saucer, Camwood Ivory shape.
5.75" dia. $2-4.

Footed bowl, Camwood Ivory shape. 3" dia. x 4.5" dia.
$6-8.

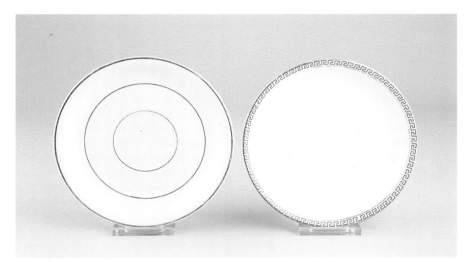

Two saucers, Camwood Ivory
shape. 5.75" dia. $2-4 ea.

Bowl, Mount Vernon shape with Universal backstamp. 2.75" h. x
6.25" dia. $6-8.

Plate, Camwood Ivory shape. 9.25" dia. $6-10.

Two bread and butter plates, Camwood Ivory shape. 6.25" dia. $3-4 ea.

Covered casserole, Universal. 3.25" h. x 9.25" dia. $28-30.

Platter, Camwood Ivory shape. 13.5" l. $14-16.

Camwood Ivory shape. Cup and saucer, 2.25" h., $8-12; platter, 10" dia., $8-12; plate, 9" dia., $6-8; pickle dish, 9" l., $8-12.

Camwood Ivory shape. Creamer, 3.75" h., $8-10; coupe soup, 7.75" dia., $4-6; fruit, 5.25" dia., $2-4; cream soup lug, 6.5" dia., $6-8; custard cup, 2.75" h., $4-6.

Graduated mixing bowls, Universal: 9" dia., $10-12; 7.5" dia., $8-10; 6" dia., $6-8; covered casserole, 3.5" h. x 8.5" dia., $18-22; Salt and pepper shakers, 4" h., $8-12.

Pie plate, Universal, 10" dia., $15-20; covered refrigerator bowl, 3.5" h. x 5" dia., $6-8; covered refrigerator bowl (missing lid), 4.5" h. x 6" dia., $8-10.

Camwood Ivory shape. Plate, bread and butter, 6.26" dia., $2-3; platter, 13.5"l., $14-16; water pitcher with ice lip, 6" h., $35-40.

Salad bowl, Universal, 3.5" h. x 9.5" dia., $18-22; salad bowl, individual (marked Ballerina), 6.75" dia., $4-8; Sugar, Camwood Ivory shape, 4" h., $10-12.

Camwood Ivory shape. Vegetable dish, 2.75" h. x 8.75" dia., $8-12; gravy boat, 8" l., $12-14; oval vegetable dish, 2" h. x 9" l., $8-12; plate, square salad, 7.25" sq., $6-8.

Camwood Ivory shape. Covered casserole, 2.5" h. x 9.5" dia., $20-24; sugar, 4" h., $10-12.

Oval vegetable dish, Old Holland Ware with Universal backstamp. 2" h. x 9.25" l., $8-12.

Left:
Platter, Old Holland Ware with Universal backstamp. 9" h. x 11.5" l., $8-12.

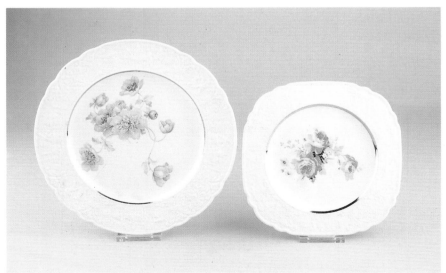

Old Holland ware with Universal backstamp. Plate, 9" dia., $6-8; plate, square salad, 7" sq., $6-8.

Camwood Ivory shape. Grill plate, 9.75" dia., $10-14; plate, 9" dia., $6-10; creamer, 3.75" h., $8-10.

Pie plate, Universal backstamp. 10" dia.. $18-22.

Camwood Ivory shape. Saucer, 5.75" dia., $2-4; creamer, 3.75" h., $8-10.

Platter, Mount Vernon shape with Universal backstamp. 11.25" sq., $14-16.

Iris decoration on Camwood Ivory shape. Plate, 9" dia., $6-8; plate, salad, 7.25" dia., $3-4; plate, bread and butter, 6" dia., $2-3; creamer, 3.75" h., $8-10.

Iris decoration on Camwood Ivory shape. Pie plate, 10" dia., $15-20; saucer, 5.25" dia., $4-5; coupe soup, 7.75" dia., $4-6; cup, 2.25" h., $4-5.

Soup tureen, Iris decoration on Camwood Ivory shape. 3.5" h. x 7.5" dia. $35-40.

Iris decoration on Mount Vernon shape. Refrigerator container with original company label, 3.5" h. x 5.25" dia., $10-14; shaker, 4.5" h., $4-5.

Detail of original company label from refrigerator container above.

Camwood Ivory shape. Saucer, 5.75" dia., $2-4; salt and pepper shakers, 4.25" h., $8-12.

Salad bowl, Universal, 3.5" h. x 9.75" dia., $16-18; water pitcher with ice lip, 6" h., $35-40.

Plate, Mount Vernon shape. 9" dia. $6-8.

Platter, Camwood Ivory shape. 8" h. x 11" l., $8-12.

Camwood Ivory shape. Oval vegetable dish, 2.25" h. x 9" l., $8-10; platter, 14.75" l., $14-16; pickle, 9.25" l., $8-12; gravy boat, 8" l., $12-14.

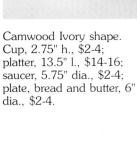

Camwood Ivory shape. Sugar, 4" h., $10-12; vegetable dish, 2.75" h. x 8.75" dia., $8-12; coupe soup, 7.75" dia.; $4-6; creamer, 3.75" h., $8-10.

Camwood Ivory shape. Cup, 2.75" h., $2-4; platter, 13.5" l., $14-16; saucer, 5.75" dia., $2-4; plate, bread and butter, 6" dia., $2-4.

Camwood Ivory shape. Platter, 11.5" dia., $12-14; teapot, 5" h., $27-32; custard cup, 2.5" h., $4-6; small bowl, 1.75" h. x 5" dia., $2-4.

Camwood Ivory shape (with gold band). Creamer, 3.75" h., $8-10; vegetable dish, 2.75" h. x 9.5" dia., $8-12; saucer, 5.75" dia., $2-4; covered casserole, 2.5" h. x 9.5" dia., $35-40; sugar, 3.75" h., $10-12.

Camwood Ivory shape. Gravy boat, 8.25" l., $12-14; platter, 10.5" h. x 13.5" l., $14-16; plate, 9.75" dia., $6-8; plate, salad, 7.25" dia., $3-4.

Camwood Ivory shape. Egg cup, 3.25" h., $14-16; vegetable dish, 2.75" h. x 9" dia., $8-12; bowl, 1.5" h. x 6" dia., $6-8; royal soup, 2.5" h. x 5" dia., $14-16; fruit, 5.25" dia., $2-4.

Camwood Ivory shape. Creamer, 3.75" h., $8-10; sugar, 4" h., $10-12; plate, bread and butter, 6.26" dia., $2-3; pickle, 9.25" l., $8-12; cup, 2.5" h., $2-4; saucer, 5.75" dia., $2-4.

Detail of border pattern applied to the edge of Camwood Ivory plate. According to Arden Kail, a former Universal liner, the liners in the decorating department hand painted the gold border. The lower line is called a verg line.

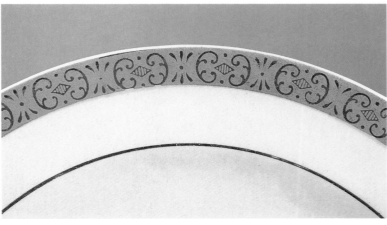

Camwood Ivory shape (with platinum band). Sugar, 4.5" h., $10-12; platter, 10.25" h. x 13.5" l., $14-16; vegetable dish, 2" h. x 9" l., $8-12.

Camwood Ivory shape (with platinum band). Platter, 9" h. x 11.5" l., $12-14; cup, 2.5" h., $2-4; saucer, 5.75" dia., $2-4; fruit, 5.25" dia., $2-4.

Camwood Ivory shape (with platinum band). Plate, salad, 7.25" dia., $3-4; creamer, 3.75" h., $8-10; plate, 9.25" dia., $6-8; plate, 9.75" dia., $6-10; plate, bread and butter, 6" h., $2-3.

Detail of platinum band applied to edge of Camwood Ivory plate.

Camwood Ivory shape. Sugar, 3.25" h., $10-12; saucer, 5.75" dia., $2-4; fruit, 5.25" dia., $2-4; teacup, 2.5" h., $2-4.

Bittersweet decoration on Camwood Ivory shape. Plate, salad, 7.25" dia., $6-8; platter, 10.5" h. x 13.5" l., $28-32; salt and pepper shakers, 3.75" h., $20-24; creamer, 3.75" h., $16-20.

Bittersweet decoration on Camwood Ivory shape. Vegetable dish, 2.5" h. x 9" dia., $16-24; coupe soup, 7.75" dia., $8-12; vegetable dish, 2.75" h. x 8.75" dia., $16-24.

Bittersweet decoration on Camwood Ivory shape. Three piece stove set: salt and pepper, 4.75" h., $16-24; grease bowl, 3.5" h., $38-42.

Bittersweet decoration on Camwood Ivory shape. Plate, 9.25" dia., $16-24; saucer, 5.75" dia., $8-10; cup, 2.5" h., $8-10.

Bittersweet decoration on Camwood Ivory shape. Stacking set (three casseroles with one top lid), 2" h. x 6.5" dia., $44-48; water jug with ice lip and lid, 6.5" h., $38-44.

Covered casserole, Bittersweet decoration on Camwood Ivory shape. 4.5" h. x 7.5" dia. $36-42.

Detail of Bittersweet decoration.

Two pieces with Netherlands Universal backstamp. Plate, 10" sq., $6-10; bowl, 1.5" h. x 6.25" dia., $4-6.

Additional pieces with Netherlands Universal backstamp. Plate, 10" sq., $6-10; coupe soup, 7.75" dia., $4-6.

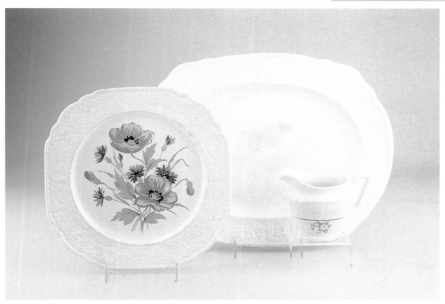

Netherlands Universal backstamp. Plate, 10" sq., $6-10; platter, 11" h. x 14.25" l., $12-14; creamer, 3.5" h., $8-10.

Plate, Netherlands Universal backstamp. 9.75" sq. $6-10.

Plate, salad, Netherlands Universal backstamp. 7" sq. $3-4.

Detail of border pattern on Netherlands Universal plate.

Netherlands Universal backstamp. Plate, 10" sq., $6-10; platter, 11.5" dia., $12-14.

Two coupe soups, Netherlands Universal backstamp. 7.75" dia., $4-6 ea.

Backstamp, Netherlands Universal.

Indian Tree decoration/pattern on Heirloom shape (with gold trim). Sugar, 4.5" h., $12-14; platter, 11.5" h. x 15" l., $14-16; salt and pepper shakers, 3" h., $10-14.

Indian Tree decoration/pattern on Heirloom shape. Plate, 10" dia., $8-12; salad bowl, individual, 2" h. x 6.75" dia., $6-8; fruit, 5.5" dia., $4-6; plate, bread and butter, 6.25" dia., $2-4.

Detail of border pattern. This application was called stencil.

Indian Tree decoration/pattern on Heirloom shape. Cup, 2.75" h.; saucer, 6.25" dia., $10-12 set.

Indian Tree decoration/pattern on Heirloom shape (without gold trim). Plate, salad, 7.25" dia., $3-4; saucer, 6.25" dia., $3-5; cup, 2.75" h., $3-5; plate, 10" dia., $8-12; plate, bread and butter, 6.25" dia., $2-3.

Indian Tree decoration/pattern on Heirloom shape. Vegetable dish, 2.75" h. x 9.25" dia., $10-14; salt and pepper shakers, 3" h., $8-14; sugar, 5" h., $12-14.

Indian Tree decoration/pattern with turkey decal on Heirloom shape. Platter, 11.5" h. x 15" l., $14-16.

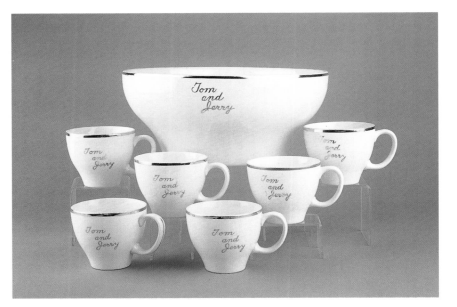

Tom and Jerry bowl with hunting theme decoration, Mount Vernon shape, Universal backstamp. 4.25" h. x 10.25" dia. $18-20.

Tom and Jerry set with six cups, unmarked. Bowl, 4.5" h. x 10.25" dia.; cups: 2.75" h.. $55-65.

Tom and Jerry set with nine cups, Upico shape, Universal backstamp. Bowl, 4.5" h. x 10.5" dia.; cups, 3" h.. $55-65.

Tom and Jerry set with six cups and hunting theme decoration, Universal backstamp. Bowl, 4.25" h. x 10 5/8" dia.; cups, 3" h. $55-65.

Tom and Jerry set with eight cups, unmarked. Bowl, 4.25" h. x 10.5" dia.; cups, 2.5" h. $55-65.

Tom and Jerry set with seven cups, Universal backstamp. Bowl, 4.25" h. x 10.25" dia.; cups, 3" h. $45-55.

Three Tom and Jerry cups, Upico shape. 3" h. $4-5 ea.

Tom and Jerry set with six cups, Upico shape, Universal backstamp. Bowl, 4.25" h. x 10.25" dia.; cups, 3" h. $45-55.

Batter set without underplate, Upico shape. Batter jug, 9" h., $45-50; syrup, 6" h., $35-40; shaker, 4.25" h., $8-10.

Batter set with underplate, Upico shape. Batter jug, 9" h.; syrup, 6" h.; shaker, 4.25" h. $80-90 set.

Assortment of water jugs, all Upico shape, four with horizontal stripes, 8" h.; one with vertical stripes, 8.5" h. $35-40 ea.

Pitchers, (two with lids), Upico Ivory Red & White Kitchenware. 6.75" h., $35-40; 4.75" h., $18-24; 7" h., $18-20.

Upico Ivory Red & White Kitchenware assortment. Salad bowl, 3.25" h. x 9" dia., $16-18; shaker, 4.5" h., $8-10; salad fork and spoon, $18-22 pr.

Assortment of Upico Ivory. Batter tray, Red & White Kitchenware, 12.5" dia., $16-18; creamer, Red & White Kitchenware, 4.5" h., $10-12; custard, Red & White Kitchenware, 2.75" h., $4-6; creamer, Black & White Kitchenware, 4.5" h., $10-12.

Upico Ivory Red & White Kitchenware assortment. Teapot, 5.5" h., $35-40; lid, 5.75" dia., $6-8; covered casserole, 3.5" h. x 8.25" dia., $28-32.

Salad fork and spoon, Universal. $18-22 pr.

Large cup and saucer with gold decoration, marked "Father." Cup, 3" h.; saucer, 7.5" dia. $18-22.

Pair of large cups and saucers with blue decoration, marked "Father" and "Mother." Cups, 3" h.; saucers, 7.25" dia. $18-22 ea.

Pair of large cups and saucers with rose decoration, marked "Father" and "Mother." Cups, 3" h.; saucers, 7.25" dia. $18-22 ea.

Two grill plates in blue and mulberry. Empress Ivory decoration (a variation of the willow pattern). 9.75" dia. $10-14 ea.

Camwood Ivory shape. Platter, 11.75" dia., $12-14; saucer, 5.75" dia., $2-4; plate, 9" dia., $6-8.

Backstamp, Empress Ivory decoration.

Camwood Ivory shape with stamped on pattern. Pepper, 4" h., $4-6; platter, 11.5" l., $12-14; custard, 3" h., $4-6.

Camwood Ivory shape. Plate, salad, 8" dia., $3-4; plate, 9.75" dia., $6-8; cream soup lug, 6.75" dia., $6-8.

Camwood Ivory shape. Plate, bread and butter, 6" dia., $2-3; fruit, 5.25" dia., $2-4; cup, 2.5" h., $2-4; saucer, 5.75" dia., $2-4.

Camwood Ivory shape. Pie plate, 8.75" dia., $15-20; mixing bowl, 3" h. x 6" dia., $6-8; coupe soup, 7.75" dia., $6-8.

Footed bowl, Camwood Ivory shape, 3" h. x 5.25" dia., $6-8; water pitcher with ice lip, 6" h., $35-40.

Grill plate, Empress Ivory. 9.75" dia. $10-14.

Two pieces in Empress Ivory. Salad bowl, 3.5" h. x 9.75" dia., $8-12; casserole (missing lid), 3.5" h. x 8.25" dia., $12-14.

Detail of design from salad bowl.

Backstamp from the Empress Ivory pieces, "Especially Made for Blair." Blair was another company that contracted with Universal to produce dinnerware.

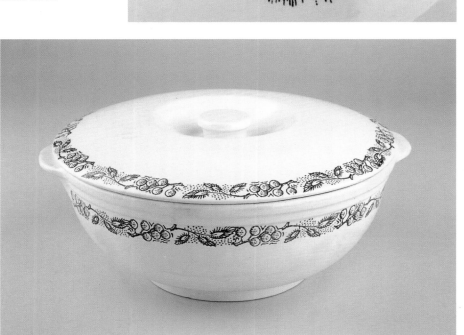

Covered casserole, Camwood Ivory shape. 3.5" h. x 8.5" dia. $16-18.

Camwood Ivory shape. Plate, 10" dia., $6-10; plate, bread and butter, 6.25" dia., $2-3; saucer, 5.75" dia., $2-4; creamer, 3.5" h., $8-10.

Detail of pattern on bread and butter plate.

Camwood Ivory shape. Coupe soup, 7.75" dia., $6-8; footed bowl, 3" h. x 5.25" dia., $6-8; fruit, 5.25" dia., $2-4.

Milk pitcher, Upico shape, 7.25" h., $18-24; salad bowl, marked "Especially Made for Blair," 3.5" h. x 9.5" dia., $16-18; water jug, marked "Oxford Ware," 8" h., $27-30.

Backstamp from salad bowl, "Especially Made for Blair."

Batter tray, 11.5" dia., $18-22; covered refrigerator bowl, Upico shape, 2.75" h. x 5.5" dia., $10-14.

Covered casserole, Upico Ivory shape. 4" h. x 8.5" dia. $28-30.

Upico Ivory shape. Casserole lid, 7.5" dia., $8-10; saucer, 5.75" dia., $3-5; plate, bread and butter, 6.25" dia., $2-3; salt and pepper shakers, 4.75" h., $8-12.

Detail of design on the Upico Ivory pieces shown above.

Backstamp, Upico Ivory shape.

Upico shape. Covered refrigerator container, 3.5" h. x 7.5" l., $18-24; butter, 1 lb., 3.5" h. x 6.25" l., $18-24.

Upico shape, different decorations. Mixing bowl, 3.75" h. x 9" dia., $14-16; custard, 2.5" h., $4-6.

Upico shape, different decorations. Plate, bread and butter, 6.25" dia., $2-4; platter, 11.25" l., $12-14.

Upico shape, different decorations. Covered casserole, 2" h. x 6.5" dia., $12-14; plate, bread and butter, 6.25" dia., $3-4.

Upico shape. Plate, 9" dia., $6-8; covered refrigerator container, 2" h. x 4.5" dia., $10-14; water jug, 9" h., $27-30.

Covered casserole, Upico shape. 3.5" h. x 8.25" dia. $18-22.

Two butter dishes, Upico shape. Butter, 1 lb., 3.5" h. x 6.25" l., $35-40; butter, 1/4 lb., 3" h. x 7" l., $14-16.

Garden Glory decoration on Upico shape. Salt and pepper shakers, 4.25" h., $8-12; plate, 9.25" dia., $6-8; creamer, 3" h., $10-12; mixing bowl, 3" h. x 6" dia., $8-12.

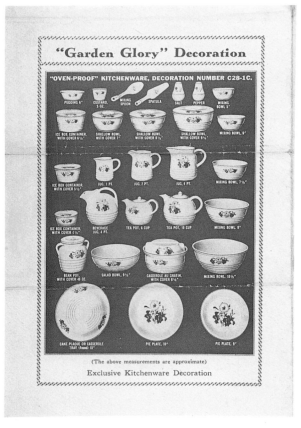

Flyer advertising Garden Glory decoration.

American Beauty Rose decoration on Upico shape. Bowl, 5.75" dia., $4-6; oatmeal, 6" dia., $4-6; teapot, 5.25" h., $35-40; coupe soup, 8" dia., $4-6.

American Beauty Rose decoration on Upico shape. Fruit, 5 1/8" dia., $2-4; gravy boat, 8" dia., $12-14; bowl, 2.5" h. x 5.25" dia., $12-14.

Coupe soup, Upico shape. 7.75" dia. $4-6.

Salt and pepper shakers, Upico Ivory. 4.75" h. $8-12.

Jug, Upico Ivory shape. 6.25" h. $20-26.

Plate, Upico Ivory shape, 10" dia., $6-10; salt and pepper shakers, 4.5" h., $8-10.

Oatmeal, Upico Ivory shape, 6" dia., $4-6; oatmeal, Camwood Ivory shape, 5.75" dia., $2-4; fruit, Upico Ivory shape, 5.25" dia., $2-4.

Sugar and creamer, Upico Ivory shape. 3" h. $10-14 ea.

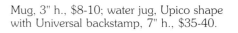

Mug, 3" h., $8-10; water jug, Upico shape with Universal backstamp, 7" h., $35-40.

Upico Ivory shape. Sugar, 4.5" h., $12-14;
oval vegetable dish, 2" h. x 9" l., $8-12; platter,
$8-12.

Upico Ivory shape. Saucer, 5.75" dia., $2-4;
plate, 9.25" dia., $6-10; plate, bread and
butter, 6.25" dia., $2-3.

Upico Ivory shape. Saucer, 5.75" dia.; cup, 2.5" h., $6-8 set.

Cream soup lug, unmarked. 7" dia. $4-6.

Assortment in Laurella shape. Plate, 9.25" dia., $6-8; plate, 10" dia., $6-10; plate, 6.5" dia., $4-6; gravy bowl, 3.5" h. x 5.5" dia., $12-14.

Laurella shape. Platter, 13.5" dia., $14-16; platter, 11.5" dia., $12-14; covered casserole, 3.25" h. x 10.25" dia., $16-22.

Laurella shape. Cup and saucer, 3" h., $8-12.; tidbit tray, 9" h., $18-22; cream soup, lug, 7" dia., $8-10; coupe soup, 7.75" dia., $4-6; salt and pepper shakers, 3.5" h., $8-12.

Laurella shape. Mixing bowl, 5" h. x 9" dia., $14-16; bowl, 3" h. x 5.5" dia., $6-8; mixing bowl, 4.5" h. x 8" dia., $12-14; sugar and creamer, 3.75" h., $12-14; nappy, 9 1/8" dia., $8-12; fruit, 5.5" dia., $2-4.

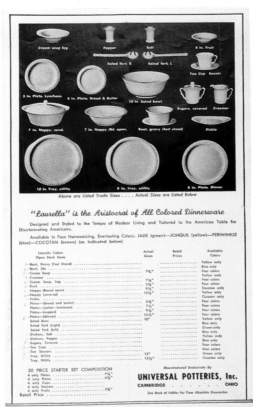

Flyer advertising dinnerware in the Laurella shape.

Teapot, American Beauty decoration on Laurella shape. 5.75" h. $35-40.

Sugar and creamer, Laurella shape. Sugar: 5.25" h., $10-12; creamer: 4.25" h., $8-10.

Plate, Laurella shape. 10.25" dia. $6-10.

Gravy boat, Laurella shape. 3.5" h. x 7.5" dia. $12-14.

Laurella shape, different decorations. Platter, 11.75" dia., $12-14; plate, 10" dia., $6-10.

Two different Laurella backstamps.

Assortment in Rodeo shape. Sugar, 4.25" h., $12-14; creamer, 3.5" h., $8-10; platter, 13.25" dia., $14-16; plate, 9 1/8" dia., $6-8; cup and saucer, 2.5" h., $8-10; coupe soup, 7.75" dia., $4-6; bowl, 6.25" dia., $6-8.

Additional Rodeo pieces. Plate, salad, 7" dia., $3-4; pickle, 9.25" l., $9-12; gravy boat, 7.75" l., $12-14; plate, bread and butter, 6.25" dia., $2-3.

Plate, Roy Rogers decoration on Rodeo shape. 9.25" dia. $35-45.

Backstamp, Rodeo shape.

Pie plates, different decorations, both with gold trim. 10" dia. $15-20 ea.

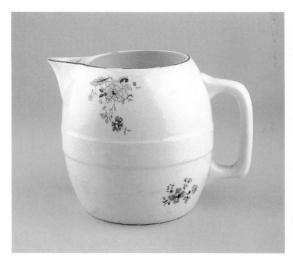

Water pitcher with ice lip, Universal. 6.5" h. $25-30.

Plate, Camwood Ivory shape, 9.25" dia., $6-8; plate, Ballerina shape, 9.25" dia., $6-8.

Plate, Ballerina shape, 9.25" dia., $6-8; Plate, Camwood Ivory shape, 9" dia., $6-8.

Plate, Ballerina shape, 10" dia., $6-8; Plate, Camwood Ivory shape, 9.75" dia., $6-8.

Two pieces marked Hill Craft by Universal. Pie plate, 8.5" dia., $15-20; salad bowl, 3.75" h. x 8.75" dia., $16-18.

Backstamp, Hill Craft by Universal.

Covered refrigerator container (with lid), Universal. 3" h. x 4.25" dia. $10-12.

Water jug, made specifically for Rotary International, with Rotary logo on top, 9" h., $35-40; vegetable dish, 3.25" h. x 9.25" dia., $16-18.

Detail of Rotary International logo on top of water jug.

Refrigerator container, Upico shape. 4" h. x 6" l. $35-40.

Two water jugs, Universal. 7.5" h. and 9" h. $35-40 ea.

Platter, Universal, 12.5" dia., $18-22; covered refrigerator container, 2.75" h. x 3.75" sq., $12-16.

Water jug, Universal Tip Top, 7.5" h., $55-60; mixing bowl, 3.75" h. x 8.25" dia., $8-12.

Backstamp from Tip Top water jug.

Kitchen Bouquet decoration on Camwood Ivory shape. Covered casserole, 3.25" h. x 8" dia., $18-22; water pitcher, 6.5" h., $35-40.

Covered refrigerator container, Kitchen Bouquet decoration on Camwood Ivory shape. 4" h. x 8" l. $18-24.

Backstamp, Kitchen Bouquet decoration.

Flyer advertising Ballerina shape items in "Outstanding Decorator Colors."

Flyer advertising two new colors in Ballerina shape.

Flyer advertising new items in Ballerina shape.

Backstamp, Ballerina.

Flyer advertising Ballerina Oven-Proof Kitchenware items, "To Match Your Ballerina Dinnerware."

Pink Dogwood decoration on Ballerina shape. Sugar, 3.25" h., $10-12; and creamer, 3.25" h., $8-10; teacup, 2" h., $2-4; saucer, 6" dia., $2-4; custard cup, 2.5" h., $4-6; fruit, 5.25" dia., $2-4; double egg cup, 4.25" h., $14-16.

Additional pieces with Pink Dogwood decoration on Ballerina shape. Back: pie plate, 10" dia., $15-20; platter, 12" dia., $12-14; plate, 10" dia., $6-10. Front: plate, bread and butter, 6.25" dia., $2-3; plate, 6.5" dia., $2-3.

Pink Dogwood decoration on Ballerina shape. Vegetable dish, 2" h. x 9" dia., $8-12; plate, 10" dia., $6-10; coupe soup, 7.75" dia., $4-6; salad bowl, individual, 7" dia., $3-4.

Ballerina shape. Vegetable dish, 2.5" h. x 9" dia., $8-12; salad bowl, 3.5" h. x 9.5" dia., $16-18.

Ballerina shape. Creamer, 3.25" h., $8-10; plate, salad, 7.25" dia., $3-4; plate, bread and butter, 6.25" dia., $2-3; oatmeal, 6" dia., $2-4.

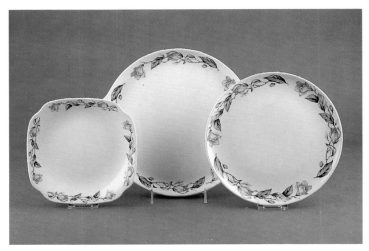

Ballerina shape. Plate, square salad, 7.25" sq., $6-8; platter, 10.5" dia., $8-12; plate, 9 1/8" dia., $6-8.

Assortment of pieces with Leaf backstamp. Back: two plates, bread and butter, 6.25" dia., $2-3 ea.; platter, 11.5" dia., $14-16; nappy, 2.5" h. x 9" dia., $8-10; fruit, 5.25" dia., $2-4. Front: two cups and saucers, 2" h., $8-10 ea.

Backstamp, Leaf shape.

Additional pieces with Leaf backstamp. Two plates, 10" dia., $6-10 ea.; sugar, 3" h., $10-12; creamer, 2.5" h., $7-9.

Largo decoration on Ballerina shape. Coupe soup, 7.75" dia., $4-6; vegetable dish, 9" l., $8-12.

Largo decoration on Ballerina shape. Salt and pepper shakers, 2.5" h., $8-12; platter, 12" dia., $12-14; plate, bread and butter, 6.25" dia., $2-4; plate, 10" dia., $6-10; refrigerator bowl, 4.5" h., 6" dia., $6-8.

Largo decoration on Ballerina shape. Teacup, 2" h., $2-4; saucer, 5.75" dia., $2-4; sugar, 3.25" h., $10-12.

Salad plate, Ballerina shape, made for Harmony House. 7.5" dia. $2-4.

Large platter with turkey decoration, Ballerina shape. 14.5" dia. $14-16.

Batter tray, 12.75" dia., $18-20; custard cup, 2.75" h., $4-6; bowl, 1.75" h. x 5" dia., $6-8; teapot, 6.5" h., $35-40.

Trade Winds decoration. Teapot, 5" h., $30-32; platter, Ballerina shape, 12" dia., $12-14; plate, bread and butter, Ballerina shape, 6" dia., $2-3; Universal nameplate, $50-60.

Plate, Ballerina shape, 9.25" dia., $6-8; sugar, Autumn Fancy decoration on Ballerina shape, 2.75" h., $10-12.

Flyer advertising Autumn Fancy decoration on Ballerina.

Ballerina shape. Platter, 13.25" dia., $6-10; platter, 11.5" dia., $6-8; gravy boat, 8" l., $12-14.

Ballerina shape. Plates: 10" dia., $6-10; 9.25" dia., $6-8; 7.5" dia., $3-4; 6.25" dia., $2-3; sugar, 3.75" h., $10-12.

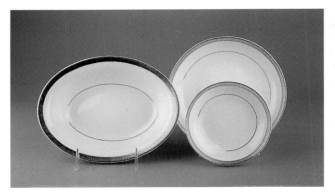

Ballerina shape. Oval vegetable dish, 2" h. x 9" l., $8-12; coupe soup, 7.25" dia., $4-6; fruit, 5.25" dia., $2-4.

Ballerina shape. Creamer, 3.25" h., $8-10; pickle, 9.25" l., $8-12; cup, 2.25" h., $2-4; saucer, 6.25" dia., $2-4.

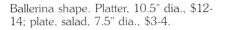

Ballerina shape. Platter, 10.5" dia., $12-14; plate, salad, 7.5" dia., $3-4.

Teacup, Bamboo decoration on Ballerina shape. 2" h. $2-4.

Flyer advertising Bamboo decoration on Ballerina.

After dinner cup and saucer, Ballerina shape with "Hardtack" design. Cup, 1.75" h.; saucer, 5.25" dia. $8-10.

Square salad plate, unmarked. 7.25" sq. $6-8.

Cup, Ballerina shape. 2.25" h. $4-5.

Creamer, Ballerina shape. 3.25" h. $8-10.

Ballerina shape. Plate, 9.25" dia., $6-8; cup, 2.25" h., $2-4; saucer, 6.25" dia., $2-4; sugar, 4.5" h., $10-12; fruit, 5.5" dia., $2-4.

Ballerina shape. Creamer, 3.5" h., $8-10; vegetable dish, 2.75" h. x 9" dia., $8-12; salt and pepper shakers, 3" h., $8-12.

Assortment of pieces with Moss Rose decoration, Ballerina backstamp. Sugar, 4.25" h., $10-12; teapot, 5.5" h., $35-40; creamer, 3.25" h., $8-10; Universal name plate, $50-60. The name Moss Rose was taken from the Rose Garden of Mrs. G. D. Agnew, wife of Universal's president.

Moss Rose decoration, Ballerina backstamp. Cup and saucer (with green trim), 2.25" h., $8-10; cup and saucer (no trim), 2.5" h., $8-10; tumbler, 5" h., $12-14; coaster (with gold trim), 5" dia., $3-5.

Moss Rose decoration, Ballerina backstamp. Plate, 10" dia., $6-10; platter, 11 5/8" dia., $12-14; cup, 2.5" h., $2-4; after dinner coffee, 1.75" h., $2-4.

Moss Rose decoration, Ballerina backstamp. Bowl, 3.25" h. x 5.25" dia., $6-8; coupe soup, 7.75" dia., $4-6; fruit (with green trim), 5.25" dia., $2-4; cream soup lug, 7" dia.. $6-8; cup, 2.25" h., $2-4.

Moss Rose decoration, Ballerina backstamp. Covered casserole, 3.75" h. x 8.5" dia., $16-22; gravy boat, 8" l., $12-14; French casserole, 2.5" h. x 5" dia., $12-14.

Moss Rose decoration, Ballerina backstamp. Nappy (with silver trim), 9" dia., $8-12; nappy (no trim), 7.75" dia., $8-10; salad bowl, 6.75" dia., $2-4; egg cup (with green trim), 4.25" h., $14-16.

Moss Rose decoration, Ballerina backstamp. Plate, bread and butter, 6" dia., $2-4; square plate, 7.5" sq., $6-8; coffee server, 8.25" h., $30-32.

Moss Rose decoration, Ballerina backstamp. Pickle dish, 9.5" l., $8-12; butter, 1 lb., 2.5" h. x 8.25" l., $14-16; mug, 3.5" h., $8-12.

"MOSS ROSE"
ON THE BALLERINA SHAPE
UNIVERSAL POTTERIES, INC., CAMBRIDGE, OHIO

Flyer advertising Moss Rose decoration on Ballerina.

Ballerina shape. Plate, 10" dia., $6-10; plate, salad, 7.5" dia., $3-4; plate, bread and butter, 6.25" dia., $2-3.

Ballerina shape. Nappy, 9" dia., $8-12; fruit, 5.25" dia., $2-4; cream soup lug, 7" dia., $6-8.

Ballerina shape. Gravy boat, 8" l., $12-14; platter, 13.25" dia., $14-16; milk pitcher, 7" h., $20-22.

Ballerina shape. Salt and pepper shakers, 3" h., $8-12; butter, 1/4 lb., 2.5" h. x 8.25" l., $14-16; water pitcher with ice lip, 8.25" h., $30-32.

Ballerina shape. Teapot, 6.25" h., $30-32; sugar, 4" h., $10-12; creamer, 3.25" h., $8-10.

Ballerina shape. Covered casserole, 3" h. x 10" dia., $16-22; pickle dish, 9.25" l., $9-12; cup and saucer, 2" h., $8-10.

Backstamp, Universal, reverse of pieces in set at left.

Bouquet decoration on Ballerina shape. Plate, 10" dia., $6-10; plate, square salad, 7.25" sq., $6-8; saucer, 6" dia., $2-4.

Backstamp, Bouquet decoration.

Ballerina shape. Teapot, 4.25" h., $30-32; salt and pepper shakers, 2.5" h., $8-12; Coffee server, large, 8" h., $32-36.

Magnolia decoration on Ballerina shape. Platter, 11 5/8" dia., $12-14; fruit, 5.25" dia., $2-4.

Magnolia decoration on Ballerina shape. Sugar, 3.5" h., $10-12; water pitcher with ice lip, 8.25" h., $30-32; cup, 2.25" h., $2-4; custard cup, 2.5" h. x 3.5" dia., $4-6.

Flyer advertising Magnolia decoration on Ballerina.

Magnolia decoration on Ballerina shape. Salad bowl, 4" h. x 9" dia., $16-18; plate, bread and butter, 6.25" dia., $2-3.

Backstamp, Carousel shape made for Harmony House.

Carousel shape made for Harmony House, with "Starfire" decoration. Vegetable dish, 2.5" h. x 9" dia., $8-12; cup, 2" h., $2-4; coupe soup, 7.75" dia., $6-8.

Backstamp, Forecast, another decoration made for Harmony House in Carousel shape.

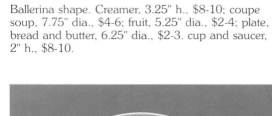

Ballerina shape. Creamer, 3.25" h., $8-10; coupe soup, 7.75" dia., $4-6; fruit, 5.25" dia., $2-4; plate, bread and butter, 6.25" dia., $2-3. cup and saucer, 2" h., $8-10.

Vegetable dish, Ballerina shape. 2.5" h. x 9" dia. $8-12.

Ballerina shape. Platter, 10.5" dia., $14-16; plate, 10" dia., $12-14; plate, 9 1/8" dia., $6-8.

Back: tumbler, 5" h., $30-32; dove gray water jug with ice lip, 8.25" h., $32-36; burgundy coffee server, 10" h., $30-32; teapot, 6.25" h., $38-42. Front: gravy boat, 8" l., $12-14; coffee server, 8.5" h., $30-32; cup and saucer, 2.25" h., $8-10; forest green grease bowl, 3.5" h., $20-22.

Stacked: platter, 11 5/8", $8-10; plates, 10" dia., $6-10; 9 1/8" dia., $6-8; 7 3/8" dia.. $3-4; plate, bread and butter, 6.25" dia., $2-3; fruit, 5.25" dia., $2-4; cream soup lug, 7" dia., $6-8; oatmeal, 6" dia., $2-4.

Covered casserole, 3" h. x 10" dia., $16-22; pickle, 9.5" l., $9-12.

Plate, bread and butter, Ballerina shape, 6.25" dia., $2-3.

Sugar, 4.25" h., $10-12; creamer, 3.25" h., $7-9.

Ballerina shape. Plate, salad, 7.25" dia., $3-4; sugar, $10-12; and creamer, $8-10, 3.25" h.

Six cup teapot, 5" h., $30-32; covered bowl, 3.5" h. x 5" dia., $12-14.

Backstamp, Universal, reverse of items shown at left.

Betsy Rose decoration on Ballerina shape, made for Harmony House. Creamer, 3.25" h., $8-10; plate, bread and butter, 6.25" dia., $2-3; saucer, 6.25" dia., $2-4; teacup, 2" h., $2-4.

Betsy Rose decoration on Ballerina shape, made for Harmony House. Plate, 10" dia., $6-10; plate, 9 1/8" dia., $6-8.

Betsy Rose decoration on Ballerina shape, made for Harmony House. Vegetable dish, 2.5" h., 9.25" dia., $8-12; salad bowl, 3.75" h. x 9.5" dia., $16-18.

Backstamp, Betsy Rose decoration.

Ballerina shape. Sugar, 4.25" h., $10-12; creamer, 3.25" h., $8-10.

Backstamp, Regency decoration on Lady Empire shape.

Regency decoration on Lady Empire shape (Ballerina). Cup and saucer, 2.5" h., $8-10; platter, 11.5" dia., $14-16; creamer, 3.5" h., $8-10.

Covered casserole with gold banding, Universal. 3.25" h. x 9" dia. $28-30.

Backstamp from the covered casserole.

Assortment of Harmony House pieces in Symphony pattern, made exclusively for Sears. Back: coffee server, A.D., 8.25" h., $32-36; teapot, 6" h., $30-32. Center: salt and pepper shakers, 3.25" h., $8-12; bowl, 3" h. x 5" dia., $6-8; tumbler with coaster, 5" h., $15-18. Front: A.D. cup and saucer, 3" h., $15-18; butter, 1/4 lb., 8" l., $14-16.

More Harmony House pieces in Symphony pattern. Coffee mug, 3.75" h., $8-12, tea cup, 4" dia., $6-8; saucer, 6.25" dia., $2-4; fruit, 5.5" dia., $2-4; plate, bread and butter, 6.25" dia., $3-5; sugar, covered, 3" h., $10-12; creamer, 3.5" h., $7-9.

Harmony House in Symphony pattern. Two nappies, 9 1/8" dia., $8-12 ea.; coupe soup, 7.75" dia., $4-6; plate, 10" dia., $6-10; egg cup, double, 4" h., $14-16.

White Peony decoration on Ballerina shape. Gravy, 8" l., $12-14; fruit, 5.5" dia., $2-4; Universal name-plate, $50-60.

Rose decoration on Ballerina shape. Sugar, 3.25" h., $10-12; saucer, 6.25" dia., $2-4; teacup, 2" h., $2-4; creamer, 3.25" h., $8-10.

Rose decoration on Ballerina shape. Coupe soup, 7.75" dia., $4-6; pickle, 9.5" l., $9-12.

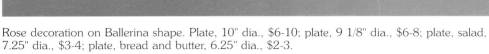

Backstamp, Rose decoration on Ballerina shape.

Rose decoration on Ballerina shape. Plate, 10" dia., $6-10; plate, 9 1/8" dia., $6-8; plate, salad, 7.25" dia., $3-4; plate, bread and butter, 6.25" dia., $2-3.

Ballerina shape. Platter, 11 5/8" dia., $12-14; plate, 10" dia., $6-10; sugar, 3.75" h., $10-12.

127

Ballerina shape. Plate, salad, 7 3/8" dia., $3-4; plate, bread and butter, 6.25" dia., $2-3; plate, 9.5" dia., $6-8; cup and saucer, 2.25" h., $8-12.

Ballerina shape. Mixing bowl, 8.5" dia., $8-12; mixing bowl, 6.25" dia., $8-10; gravy boat, 7" l., $12-14.

Ballerina shape. Platter, 14" l., $14-16; platter, 11.5" l., $12-14; salt and pepper shakers, 3.5" h., $8-12.

Ballerina shape. Salad bowl, 9.5" dia., $16-18; covered casserole, 3.5" h. x 8.5" dia., $16-22; underplate, 8.75" dia., $12-14.

Six pint water pitcher, Ballerina backstamp. 7.25" h. $35-40.

Ballerina shape. Nappy, 9" dia., $8-12; fruit, 5.5" dia., $2-4; butter, 1 lb., 3" h. x 8.25" l., $14-16.

Backstamp, Ballerina.

Ballerina backstamp. Coffee server, 9.75" h., $22-26; sugar, 3.5" h., $10-12; creamer, 4.5" h., $8-10; teapot, 6.75" h., $22-26.

Ballerina shape. Plate, 10" dia., $6-10; sugar, $10-12; and creamer, $8-10, 3.25" h.; teacup, 2" h., $2-4.

Ballerina shape. Plate, 10" dia., $6-10; gravy, 8" l., $12-14.

Ballerina shape. Plate, bread and butter, 6.25" dia., $2-3; sugar, 4" h., $10-12; cup, 2" h., $2-4.

Ballerina shape. Plate, bread and butter, 6.25" dia., $2-3; salt and pepper shakers, 3" h., $8-12; platter, 11.75" dia., $12-14; cream soup lug, 6 7/8" dia., $6-8; fruit, 5.5" dia., $2-4.

Ballerina Platinum. Pie plate, 9.5"
dia., $18-20; plate, bread and butter,
6" dia., $2-3; vegetable dish, 2.25" h.,
9" dia., $8-10; butter, 1/4 lb., $14-16.

Ballerina Platinum. Covered refrigerator bowl,
4.5" h. x 5.75" dia., $12-14; large mixing bowl,
4.25" h. x 8.5" dia., $10-14; mixing bowl,
3.75" h. x 6.5" dia., $8-10.

Ballerina Platinum. Teapot, 4.5" h., $30-32;
coffee server, 7.25" h., $32-36; milk pitcher,
6.75" h., $14-18.

Ballerina Platinum. Salad bowl, 3.5" h. x 9.5" dia., $18-22; water jug with ice lip, 7" h., $35-40.

Covered casserole, Ballerina Platinum. 3.25" h. x 8" dia., $28-32.

Backstamp, Ballerina Platinum.

Ballerina Platinum. Cup, 2.5" h., $2-4; saucer, 6.25" dia., $2-4; fruit, 5" dia., $2-4; gravy boat, 6.25" l., $12-14.

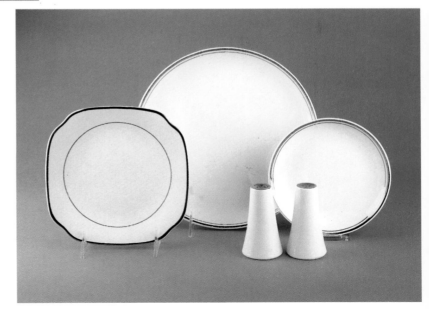

Ballerina Platinum. Square salad plate, 7.25" sq., $6-8; plate, 10" dia., $6-10; plate, bread and butter, 6.25" dia., $2-3; salt and pepper shakers, 3.75" h., $8-12.

Ballerina Mist. Back: salad bowl, 6.75" dia., $8-10; coupe soup, 7.75" dia., $4-6; pie plate, 10" dia., $15-20. Front: creamer, 3.25" h., $7-9; sugar, 3.75" h., $10-12; cup and saucer, 2.25" h., $8-10.

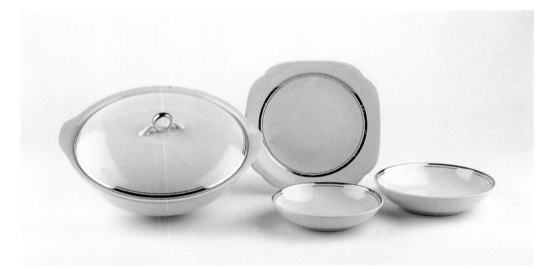

Ballerina Mist. Covered casserole, 3" h. x 9.25" dia., $16-22; square salad plate, 7.25" sq., $6-8; oatmeal, 6" dia., $2-4; fruit, 5.25" dia., $2-4.

Ballerina Mist. Covered refrigerator bowl, 4" h. x 5" dia., $8-12; covered refrigerator bowl, 5" h. x 6" dia., $12-14; covered refrigerator bowl, 3.5" h., 4" dia., $6-12; milk pitcher, 7.25" h., $18-22.

Gravy boat, 7.5" l., $12-14; pickle, 9.25" l., $9-12.

Southern Gardens decoration on Ballerina shape. Platter, 11.5" dia., $14-16; sugar, 4" h., $10-12; Universal name plate, $50-60.

Southern Gardens decoration on Ballerina shape. Saucer, 6.25" dia., $2-3; plate, 10" dia., $6-10; plate, bread and butter, 6.25" dia., $2-3.

Southern Gardens decoration on Ballerina shape. Bowl, 3.25" h. x 5.25" dia., $6-8; cream soup lug, 7" dia., $6-8; gravy, 7.75" l., $12-14.

Southern Gardens decoration on Ballerina Mist. Plate, 10" dia., $6-10; sugar, 4" h., $10-12; teacup, 2" h., $4-6; creamer, 3.25" h., $7-9.

Flyer advertising Southern Gardens decoration on Ballerina.

Strawflower decoration on Ballerina Mist. Platter, 13.25" dia., $14-16; cup and saucer, 2" h., $8-10; creamer, 3" h., $7-9; tidbit tray, 13" h., $18-22.

Strawflower decoration on Ballerina Mist. Plate, bread and butter, 6.25" dia., $2-3; coupe soup, 7.75" dia., $4-6; bowl, 3" h. x 5" dia., $6-8; Universal nameplate, $50-60; covered casserole, 3" h. x 10" dia., $16-22.

Flyer advertising Strawflower decoration on Ballerina Mist.

Ballerina Mist. Back: coupe soup, 7.75" dia., $4-6; platter, 13.25" dia., $14-16; plate, bread and butter, 6.25" dia., $2-3; platter, 11 5/8" dia., $12-14; plate, salad, 7 3/8" dia., $3-4. Front: cup and saucer, 2.5" h., $8-10; fruit, 5.25" dia., $2-4; sugar, 4.25" h., $10-12; creamer, 3/25" h., $7-9.

Ballerina Mist. Plate, 10" dia., $6-10; covered casserole, 3" h. x 10" dia., $16-22; coffee server, 8.25" h., $30-32.

Rose Corsage decoration on Ballerina Mist. Nappy, 7.75" dia., $8-10; creamer, 3.25" h., $7-9; sugar, 4" h., $10-12; nappy, 9 1/8" dia., $8-12; plate, salad, 7 3/8" dia., $3-4; salt shaker, 2.5" h., $4-6.

Rose corsage decoration on Ballerina Mist. Cup and saucer, 2" h., $8-10; cream soup lug, 6 7/8" dia., $6-8; fruit, 5.25" dia., $2-4.

Flyer advertising Rose Corsage decoration on Ballerina.

Ballerina Mist. Back: plate, 10" dia., $6-10; plate, bread and butter, 6.25" dia., $2-3; nappy, 7.25" dia., $8-12; fruit, 5.25" dia., $2-3. Front: cup and saucer, 2" h., $8-10; sugar, 4.5" h., $10-12; creamer, 3.25" h., $7-9; salt and pepper shakers, 2.75" h., $8-12.

Plate, bread and butter, Starmint decoration on Ballerina Mist shape, 6.25" dia., $2-4;
Universal nameplate, $50-60.

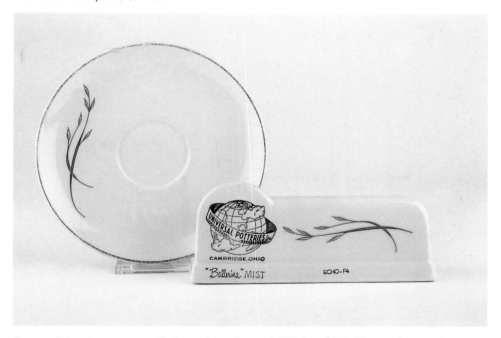

Saucer, Echo decoration on Ballerina Mist shape, 6.25" dia., $2-4; Universal nameplate,
$50-60.

Flyer advertising Echo decoration on Ballerina Mist.

Flyer advertising Butterfly decoration on Ballerina Mist.

Far left:
Coupe soup, Coral Bell decoration on Ballerina Mist shape, made for Harmony House. 7.75" dia. $6-8.

Left:
Backstamp, Coral Bell decoration on Ballerina Mist.

Far left:
Vegetable dish, Gloria decoration on Ballerina Mist shape, made for Harmony House. 2.5" h. x 9" dia. $8-12.

Left:
Backstamp, Gloria decoration on Ballerina Mist.

Platter, Ballerina Mist shape. 10.5" dia. $8-12.

Cream soup lug, Ballerina Mist shape. 6.5" dia. $6-8.

Ballerina Mist, different decorations. Sugar, 3"
h., $10-12; teacup, 2.25" h., $2-4.

Platter, Ballerina Mist shape. 10.5" dia. $8-12.

Fruit, Ballerina Mist shape. 5.25" dia. $2-4.

Ballerina Mist shape. Creamer, 3.25" h., $8-10;
salt and pepper shakers, 2.5" h., $8-12.

Ballerina Mist, different decorations. Vegetable plate, 2.5" h. x 9" dia., $8-12; plate, bread and butter, 6.25" dia., $2-4.

Vegetable dish, Iris decoration on Ballerina Mist shape, 2.5" h. x 9" dia., $8-12; salad bowl, individual, Morning Glory decoration on Ballerina Mist shape, 6.75" dia., $2-4.

Snack plate, Ballerina Mist shape, marked Atlas Tile and Marble Works, Inc. on reverse. 8.25" dia. $6-8.

Backstamp, Atlas Tile and Marble Works, Inc.

Harvest decoration on Ballerina shape (with gold trim). Fruit, 5.25" dia., $2-4; plate, bread and butter, 6" dia., $2-3; plate, 10" dia., $6-10; milk pitcher, 7" h., $20-22; pepper, 3" h., $4-6.

Harvest decoration on Ballerina shape (with gold trim). Covered casserole, 3" h. x 9.25" dia., $16-22; custard cup, 2.75" h., $2-4; small refrigerator bowl, 3" h. x 4" dia., $4-5.

Harvest decoration on Ballerina shape (with gold trim). Cream soup lug, 7" dia., $6-8; platter, 13.25" dia., $14-16; cup, 2.25" h., $2-4.

Backstamp, Harvest decoration on Ballerina shape.

Harvest decoration on Ballerina shape (with gold trim). Sugar, $10-12; and creamer, $8-10, 3.25" h.; pie plate, 10" dia., $15-20; vegetable dish, 2.75" h., 9" dia., $8-12.

141

Lady Empire decoration on Ballerina shape. Back: coffee server, A.D., 6.75" h., $30-32; plate, 10" dia., $6-10. Front: cup and saucer, 2" h., $8-10; sugar, 3" h., $8-12; salt and pepper shakers, 2.5" h., $8-12.

Lady Empire decoration on Ballerina shape. Fruit, 5.25" dia., $2-4; plate, salad, 7.25" dia., $3-4; plate, bread and butter, 6.25" dia., $2-3; creamer, 3.25" h., $8-10.

Covered casserole, Lady Empire decoration on Ballerina shape. 3" h. x 9.25" dia. $16-22.

Lady Empire decoration on Ballerina shape. Large vegetable dish, 2.5" h. x 9" dia., $8-12; vegetable dish, 2.25" h. x 7.75" dia., $8-10; coupe soup, 7.75" dia., $4-6.

Backstamp, Lady Empire decoration.

142

Thistle decoration on Ballerina shape. Plate, 10" dia., $6-10; plate, salad, 7" dia., $2-4; plate, bread and butter, 6.25" dia., $2-4.

Thistle decoration on Ballerina shape. Vegetable dish, 2.5" h. x 9" dia., $8-12; fruit, 5.25" dia., $2-4; coupe soup, 7.75" dia., $4-6.

Thistle decoration on Ballerina shape. Platter, 12" dia., $14-16; gravy boat, 8" l., $14-16.

Flyer advertising Thistle decoration on Ballerina.

Thistle decoration on Ballerina shape. Teapot, 4.5" h., $30-32; sugar, $10-12; and creamer, $8-10, 3.25" h.; cup and saucer, 2" h., $8-10.

Assortment of Cattail in green decoration. Saucer, Ballerina shape, 6.25" dia., $4-6; plate, bread and butter, Carousel shape, 6.25" dia., $4-6; coupe soup, Ballerina shape, 7.5" dia., $4-6.

Backstamp, Cattail decoration

Backstamp, Universal Cattail.

Ballerina shape. Plate, 10" dia., $6-10; cream soup, lug, 6.25" dia., $6-8.

Wood Vine decoration on Ballerina shape. Salt and pepper shakers, 2.5" h., $8-12; pickle, 9.25" l., $8-12; milk pitcher, 7" h., $20-22.

Set of nesting bowls, Wood Vine decoration on Ballerina shape. 3.25", 4", and 4.5" h. $32-38.

Wood Vine decoration on Ballerina shape. Large platter, 12.25" dia., $12-14; platter, 10.5" dia., $8-12; plate, bread and butter, 6.25" dia., $2-3; plate, salad, 7.5" dia., $3-4; fruit, 5.5" dia., $2-4.

Wood Vine decoration on Ballerina shape. Plate, 10" dia., $6-10; water jug with ice lip, 7.25" h., $35-40; cup and saucer, 2" h., $8-10.

Wood Vine decoration on Ballerina shape. Back: salad bowl, 3.5" h. x 9.75" dia., $16-18. Front: vegetable dish, 2.5" h. x 9.25" dia., $8-12; coupe soup, 7.75" dia., $4-6; salad bowl, individual, 6.75" dia., $4-6; oatmeal, 6" dia., $2-4.

Ballerina shape. Creamer, 3.25" h., $8-10; plate, bread and butter, 6.25" dia., $2-3.

Covered casserole, Universal backstamp. 3.5" h. $28-30.

Holiday theme decoration on Ballerina shape. Plate, 9.75" dia., $10-12; cup, 2" h., $4-6; saucer, 6" dia., $4-6.

Pie plate, Universal backstamp, 8.5" dia., $13-18; milk pitcher, Universal backstamp, 6.75" h., $30-36.

Platter, Ballerina shape. 10.75" dia. $8-12.

Madeira decoration on Ballerina shape. Cup and saucer, 2.25" h., $8-12; plate, bread and butter, 6.25" dia., $2-3; sugar, 3" h., $10-12.

Madeira decoration on Ballerina shape. Large platter, 12" dia., $14-16; plate, 9.25" dia., $6-8; platter, 10.75" dia., $12-14.

Ballerina shape. Platter, 12" dia., $12-14; sugar, $10-12; and creamer, $8-10, 3.25" h.; cup and saucer, 2.25" h., $8-10; teapot, 5.25" h., $30-32.

Ballerina shape. Plate, bread and butter, 6.25" dia., $2-3; plate, salad, 7.5" dia., $3-4; coupe soup, 7.75" dia., $4-6; gravy boat, 7.75" l., $12-14.

147

Ballerina shape. Pickle, 9.5" l., $9-12; plate, square salad, 7.25" sq., $6-8; butter, 1/4 lb. (missing bottom), $14-16.

Ballerina shape. Platter, 10.75" dia., $8-12; large platter, 12" dia., $12-14; gravy boat, 7.75" l., $12-14.

Ballerina shape. Sugar, $10-12; and creamer, $8-10, 3.25" h.; plate, 10" dia., $6-10; saucer, 6.25" dia., $2-4.

Milk pitcher, 6" h., $20-22; cup, Hazelnut decoration on Ballerina shape, 2" h., $2-4.

Flyer advertising Hazelnut decoration on Ballerina.

The New *APPLE* Pattern
ON THE BALLERINA SHAPE
UNIVERSAL POTTERIES, INC.
CAMBRIDGE, OHIO

"Pine Cone"
ON THE BALLERINA SHAPE
UNIVERSAL POTTERIES, INC., CAMBRIDGE, OHIO

Primrose
ON THE
BALLERINA SHAPE

UNIVERSAL POTTERIES, INC.
CAMBRIDGE, OHIO

Flyers advertising other decorations on Ballerina: Apple, Primrose, Roxanna, and Pine Cone.

Roxanna ON THE BALLERINA SHAPE
UNIVERSAL POTTERIES, INC., CAMBRIDGE, OHIO

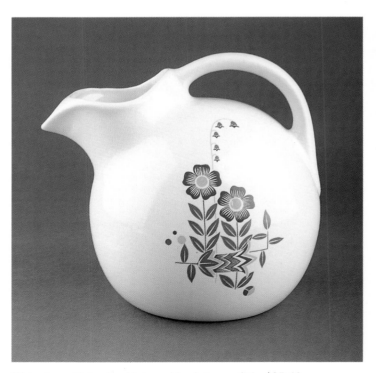

Water jug with ice lip, Universal backstamp. 6" h. $35-40.

Morning Glory decoration on Leaf shape. Two luncheon plates, 10" dia., with cups, 2.25" h. One white background, one in mist. $14-18 ea.

Two luncheon plates, Leaf shape, called "Leaf Fantasy Video Set." Colors are Elm Green and Maple Yellow. 10" dia., with cups, 2.25" h. $12-16 ea.

Four luncheon plates, Leaf shape. Colors, from top to bottom: Maple Yellow, Beach Beige, Elm Green, Linden Gray. 10" dia. $10-12 ea.

Backstamp, Leaf shape.

Leaf shape with Baby's Breath decoration on Ballerina Mist. Luncheon plate, 10" dia., with cup, 2.25" h., $10-14; Universal name plate, $50-60.

Flyer advertising Baby's Breath decoration on Ballerina Mist.

Ballerina MIST

IN THE BABY'S BREATH DECORATION

The delicate simplicity of Oriental decor is captured charmingly . . . in jet black and pure white . . . on the incredibly stable surface of Ballerina MIST, which is solid color throughout, under a crystal glaze, truly a dinnerware with a permanent pattern that will not fade or discolor.

Vogue shape. Back: plate, Mist Green, 9.5" dia., $10-14; plate, Stairway to the Stars decoration, 9.5" dia., $12-16; plate, Coffee Brown, 9.5" dia., $10-14. Front: plate, bread and butter, 6 1/8" dia., $6-8; fruit, 5 1/8" dia., $4-6; sugar, 3.25" h., $12-14.

Backstamp, Vogue shape.

Backstamp, Stairway to the Stars on Vogue.

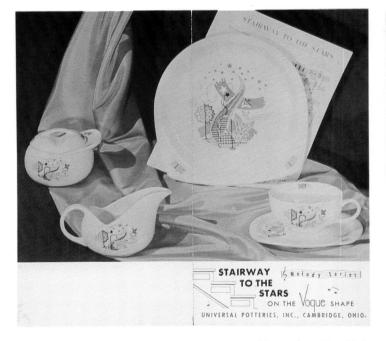

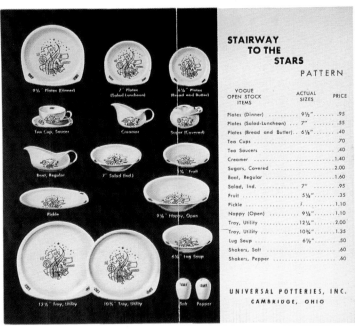

Flyer advertising Stairway to the Stars on Vogue.

Flyers advertising additional decorations on the Vogue shape: My Blue Heaven, Stormy Weather, Red Sails in the Sunset, Betty Co-ed, Moonlight & Roses.

My Blue Heaven
ON THE Vogue SHAPE
UNIVERSAL POTTERIES, INC., CAMBRIDGE, OHIO

Stormy Weather
ON THE Vogue SHAPE
UNIVERSAL POTTERIES, INC., CAMBRIDGE, OHIO

Red Sails In The Sunset
ON THE Vogue SHAPE
UNIVERSAL POTTERIES, INC., CAMBRIDGE, OHIO

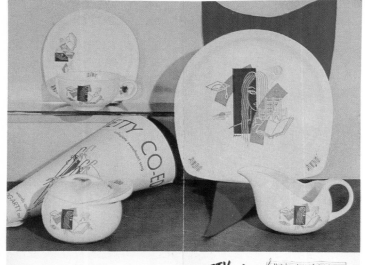

BETTY CO-ED
ON THE Vogue SHAPE
UNIVERSAL POTTERIES, INC., CAMBRIDGE, OHIO

MOONLIGHT & ROSES
ON THE Vogue SHAPE
UNIVERSAL POTTERIES, INC., CAMBRIDGE, OHIO

Shangri-La decoration on Raymor shape. Vegetable dish, 3.25" h., $10-14; creamer, 5" h., $9-12; pickle, 10.5" l., $10-14; gravy boat, 9" l., $12-14.

Backstamp, Shangri-La decoration.

Golden Burst decoration on Raymor shape. Back: large platter, 13.5" x 15.5", $16-18; platter, 12" x 13.5", $14-16. Front: sugar, 2.5" h., $12-14; creamer, 5" h., $9-12; bowl, 6.5" dia., $4-6; gravy boat, 9" l., $12-14.

Backstamp, Golden Burst decoration.

Golden Burst decoration on Raymor shape. Plate, 10" dia., $8-12; plate, bread and butter, 6.5" dia., $4-6; plate, 8.25" dia., $4-6; cup and saucer, 2.75" h., $10-12; pickle, 10.5" l., $10-14; vegetable dish, 3.25" h., $10-14.

153

Backstamp, Raymor Universal.

Salad bowl, Raymor shape. 3.75" h. x 13.25" l. $10-14.

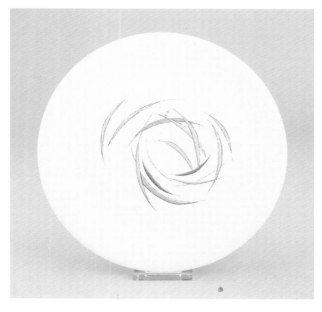

Plate, Sans Souci decoration on Raymor shape. 8.5" dia. $3-4.

Backstamp, Sans Souci decoration.

Backstamp, Stardust on Fascination.

Stardust in gray, blue, and pink on Fascination shape. Back: plate, salad, 8.25" dia., $3-4; plate, bread and butter, 6.5" dia., $3-4. Front: cup, 2.75" h., $6-8; sugar, 2.5" h., $8-12; two creamers, 5" h., $6-8 ea.

Plymouth decoration on Fascination shape. Platter, 13" h. x 14.5" l., $14-16; cream soup, 6.75" dia., $6-8; vegetable dish, 3" h., $8-12; Universal nameplate, $50-60.

Backstamp, Park Avenue decoration on Fascination.

Park Avenue decoration on Fascination shape. Back: platter, 12" l., $12-14; plate, 10" dia., $6-10. Front: gravy boat, 9" l., $12-14; pickle, 10.25" l., $9-12; sugar, 3.5" h., $8-12; creamer, 5.25" h., $6-8.

155

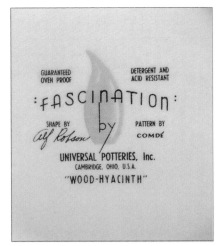

Fascination shape, various decorations. Divided vegetable dish, 4" h., $12-14; creamer, Morning Glory decoration, 5" h., $6-8; plate, 10" dia., $6-10; teapot, Wood Hyacinth decoration, 6" h., $32-38.

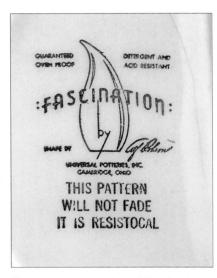

Backstamp, a variation of Fascination.

Alpine decoration on Fascination shape. Plate, 10.25" dia., $6-10; cup and saucer, 2.5" h., $8-10; soup bowl, 7" dia., $6-8.

Alpine decoration on Fascination shape. Salad bowl, 13" dia., $15-18; creamer, 5" h., $6-10.

Fruit, Fascination shape. 5.5" dia. $2-4.

Cherrytone color on Fascination shape. Covered casserole, 3" h. x 10.5" l., $16-24; pitcher, 9.5" h., $16-24.

Carousel shape. Vegetable dish, 2.75" h. x 9" dia., $10-14; cup, 2" h., $3-5.

Carousel shape. Three plates, 10" dia., $8-10 ea.; cup, 2" h., saucer, 6.25" dia., $10-12.

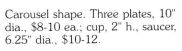

Carousel shape. Plate, bread and butter, 6.26" dia., $3-4; platter, 11.25" dia., $14-16; cream soup lug, 7" dia., $6-8.

Carousel shape. Plate, 10" dia., $8-10; cup, 2" h., $4-6.

Carousel smooth **underglaze colors**

add a wonderful touch of beauty to this fine dinnerware. All colors . . . delightfully assorted to mix or match . . . are applied UNDER THE GLAZE itself to assure permanent, perfect smoothness.

CAROUSEL OPEN STOCK ITEMS	Minimum Retail Price DENVER & WEST	
1. Gravy Boat	$1.90	
2. Bowl (Utility) 1 pint	.85	
3. Coupe Soup	.80	
4. Creamer	1.25	
5. Dessert Dish	.45	
6. Cream Soup	.55	
7. Medium Vegetable Dish (9")	1.25	
8. Handled Vegetable Dish (9½")	1.95	
9. Covered Vegetable Dish (9½")	3.75	
10. Relish Tray	1.00	
11. Bread & Butter Plate	.50	
12. Salad Plate	.55	
13. Dinner Plate	.95	
14. Salt Shaker	.75	
15. Pepper Shaker	.75	
16. Sugar	1.95	
17. Cup	.65	
18. Saucer	.40	
19. Medium Chop Plate (10½")	1.50	
20. Large Chop Plate (12½")	2.15	

16 PIECE STARTER SET-FOR-FOUR:
4—Dinner Plates   4—Cups
4—Salad Plates   4—Saucers   7.50

BERMUDA PINK • CARIBBEAN BLUE • JAMAICA GRAY • NASSAU GREEN

Flyer advertising Carousel.

Set of six coasters with original box, Fascination shape, monogrammed with letter "M." 4" dia. $30-35 box.

Assortment of six coasters, Fascination shape, three monogrammed, one plain, one with the initials "L.C.H.S" (Lore City High School). 4" dia. $4-5 ea.

Three coasters, Orchard, Paisley, and Windward decorations on Fascination shape. 4" dia. $4-5 ea.

Backstamp, Orchard decoration on Fascination shape.

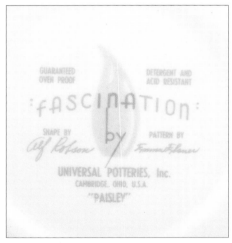

Backstamp, Paisley decoration on Fascination shape.

Backstamp, Windward decoration on Fascination shape.

Pair of ashtrays from 1952 with political theme, "We do have a choice under our flag." 5.75" dia. $12-16 ea.

Backstamp from ashtrays with political theme.

Three ashtrays with Braille alphabet and cane in center. 6" dia. $14-16 ea.

Three ashtrays with Braille alphabet and guide dog in center. 6" dia. $14-16 ea.

Assortment of advertising ashtrays. 5.75" dia. $12-16 ea.

Backstamp from Camwood Ivory ashtrays.

Assortment of ashtrays on Camwood Ivory shape. 5" dia. $12-16 ea.

Two ashtrays, one with letters "AG" intertwined in center, the other commemorating the Scottish Rite Centennial, 1857-1957. 7.25" dia. $10-14 ea.

Unusual style ashtray, flat bottom. 5" dia. $6-8.

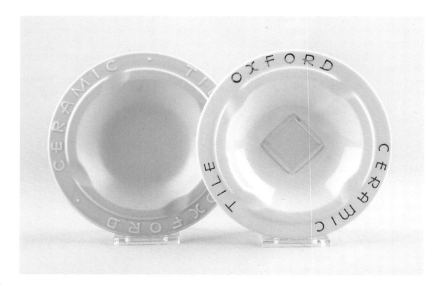

Two ashtrays made by Oxford Tile. 5.75" dia. $10-12 ea.

Grecian Urn decoration on Laurella plates, fitted with Farberware trim. Tray, 16.25" dia., $55-65; basket, 13.25" dia., $45-55.

Backstamp from Laurella plates with Farberware trim.

Grecian Urn decoration on Laurella plate, fitted with Farberware trim. 16.5" dia. $45-50.

Three sizes of bowls made for the Towle Sterling company. Bowls were shipped to Chicago from Cambridge; the lids were then fitted in Chicago. Large bowl, 5.75" h., 8.5" dia., $10-12; medium bowl, 3.75" h. x 6.75" dia., $8-10; small bowl, 3" h. x 2.25" dia., $6-8.

Three plates with bird decorations and red border. 8.25" dia.. $10-12 ea.

Three square salad plates, crab, shrimp, and lobster decorations on Camwood Ivory shape. 7.25" sq. $6-8 ea.

Two square plates, chicken/vegetable and fruit decorations on Camwood Ivory shape. 7.25" sq. $6-8 ea.

Three plates with religious theme, Ballerina shape. 9.25" dia., $8-12 ea.

Two decorative plates, Camwood Ivory shape. 11" dia. $20-24 ea.

Souvenir plates, "Souvenir of Cambridge Ohio / Sesquicentennial / 1798 / 1948," Laurella shape. Platter, 11.75" dia., $18-24; plate, 10" dia., $16-20.

Platter, Ballerina shape, "Muskingum College, Brown Chapel." 11.5" dia. $8-12.

Water jug with ice lip, Empress Ivory backstamp, made exclusively for the Cambridge Country Club. $40-50.

Detail of water jug decoration, showing the Cambridge Country Club.

Detail of water jug handle.

Pizza plate, Ballerina backstamp. 11.25" dia. $18-22.

Plate, Camwood Ivory, advertising "Oven Proof Dinnerware & Kitchenware. Free with Cash Purchases." 10" dia. $38-42.

Assortment in Wigwam decoration. Plate, bread and butter, Carousel shape, 6.25" dia., $6-8; ashtray, 6" dia., $12-16; Plate, Carousel shape, 10" dia., $10-14; cream soup lug, Ballerina shape, 7" dia., $8-12.

Tom and Jerry bowl, Universal backstamp, 4.25" h. x 10.5" dia., $18-22; water jug, 6" h., $35-40.

Canasta card holder, Universal backstamp. 4" h. x 6" w. $50-55.

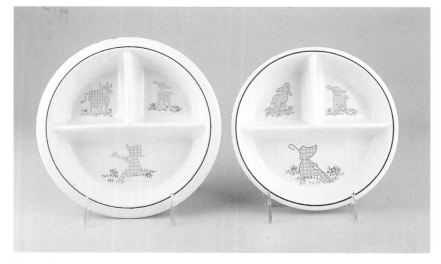

Two children's feeding dishes, Juvenile Ware, "Boy Blue" and "Bo Peep." 7.25" dia. $22-26 ea.

Backstamp, Juvenile Ware.

Assortment of Juvenile Ware. "Jack and Jill" theme. Bowl, 5.25" dia., $6-8; plate, 7 1/8" dia., $4-6; mug, 2.75" h., $18-20.

Additional Juvenile Ware pieces. Mug, 2.75" h., $18-20; plate, 7.25" dia., $4-6.

Juvenile Ware mug. "Little Boy Blue." 3" h. $18-20.

Set of five children's mugs made for the Borden Company, including "Elmer" (two versions), "Elsie" (two versions), and Beauregard. 3" h. $35-45 ea.

Backstamp from the "Beauregard" mug.

Universal nameplate, Spring Garden decoration on Ballerina. $50-60.

Universal nameplate, Gaiety decoration on Ballerina. $50-60.

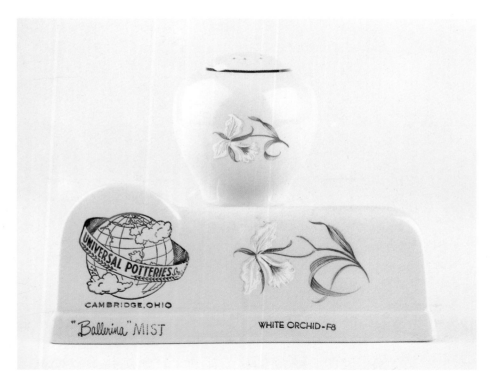

Salt shaker, White Orchid decoration on Ballerina Mist shape, 2.5" h., $4-6; Universal nameplate, $50-60.

Universal nameplate, Spring Garden on Ballerina Mist. $50-60.

Universal nameplate, Sylvan on Ballerina Mist. $50-60.

Universal nameplate, Snowdrop on Ballerina Mist. $50-60.

Commemorative plate. Universal. marked "1836-1936 Texas Under Six Flags," 6" dia.. $18-22; matching water jug. 7" h., $55-75.

Detail of commemorative plate.

Pair of large cups in pastel colors. 3" h. $6-8 ea.

Pitcher, unmarked, possibly an experimental piece. 9" h., $45-50.

Two Knife Aid knife sharpeners. 11.25" l. $18-20 ea.

Dinnerware pieces used by organizations and churches, Camwood Ivory shape. Plate, marked "I.O.O.F. / F.L.T." (Odd Fellows), 9" dia., $6-8; plate, marked "1st U.P.," 9" dia., $6-8; two teacups, marked "M.C.," 2.25" h. and 2.5" h., $2-4 ea.

Plate, bread and butter, Mount Vernon shape, used by church, marked "M.C." 6" dia. $2-3.

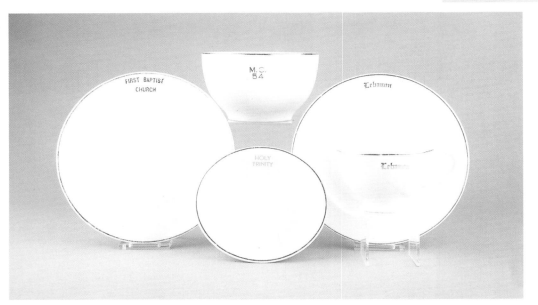

Additional dinnerware pieces used by organizations and churches, Camwood Ivory shape. Plate, marked "First Baptist Church," 7.25" dia., $3-4; bowl, marked "M.C. 54," 3" h. x 5" dia., $6-8; fruit, marked "Holy Trinity," 5.25" dia., $2-4; plate, marked "Lebanon," 7.25" dia., $3-4; cup, marked "Lebanon," 2.5" h., $2-4.

Detail of State Highway Patrol decal.

Two plates with "State Highway Patrol / Ohio / 1933-1958" decal, Ballerina Mist shape. Plate, 10" dia., $8-12; plate, bread and butter, 7.5" dia., $4-8.

Three butter pats, Ballerina Mist shape, center marked Lady Empire on reverse, right marked "1960 L.C.H.S." on front (Lore City High School). 3.25" dia. $3-5 ea.

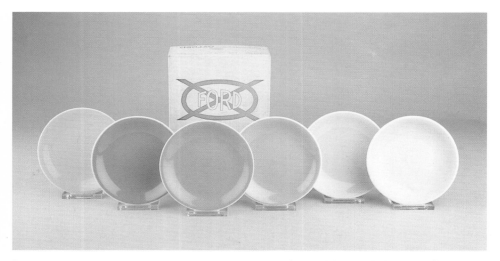

FINE TASTE
IN WALLS
OXFORD
CERAMIC TILE

Set of coasters with original box, showing colors manufactured by the Oxford Tile Company, a late 1950s division of Universal Potteries. $30-35 box.

Backstamp from Oxford Tile coasters.

Box originally used to hold red tinting for dinnerware, 1947.

Detail of label on side of red tinting box.

FRAGILE
MADE IN U.S.A.

#465-9 PC.
TOM & JERRY
SET
7. PC.

Seven piece Tom and Jerry set in original Universal box.

DINNERWARE KITCHENWARE
FROM
UNIVERSAL
POTTERIES,
INC.
CAMBRIDGE, OHIO

Reverse of Tom and Jerry box, showing Universal label.

Original ware box, 1940s-50s. Stamp on side indicates box was from Plant 2.

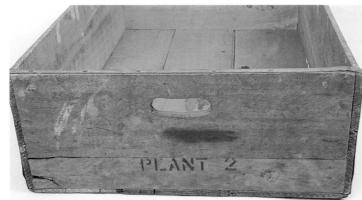

Detail of stamp on box.

Ware basket, used to carry greenware to the kiln, c. 1940s. 13.25" h. x 27" dia.

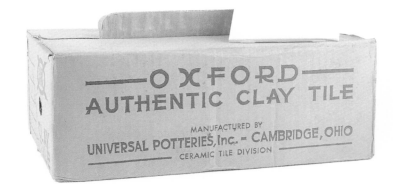

Original box of ceramic tiles from Oxford, the 1950s ceramic tile division of Universal Potteries.

Index

Advertising
Apple, 149
Autumn Fancy, 112
Butterfly, 137
Carousel, 158
Garden Glory, 97
Hazelnut, 148
Laurella, 101
Moss Rose, 117
Pine Cone, 149
Primrose, 149
Rose Corsage, 136
Roxanna, 149
Thistle, 143
Vogue, Betty Co-ed, 152
Vogue, Moonlight & Roses, 152
Vogue, My Blue Heaven, 152
Vogue, Red Sails in the Sunset, 152
Vogue, Stormy Weather, 152

Backstamps
American Beauty Rose, 65
Ballerina Platinum, 132
Betsy Rose, 125
Bouquet, 120
Broadway Rose, 33
Calico Fruit, 45
Cambridge Ivory, A.G.C. Co., 30
Camwood Ivory, 46
Camwood Ivory Cattail, 62
CAP/Guernsey Cooking Ware, 11
Edgewood, 17
Empress Ivory, 90
Fascination, Orchard, 159
Fascination, Paisley, 159
Fascination, Park Avenue, 155
Fascination, Stardust, 154
Fascination, Windward, 159
Fascination, Wood Hyacinth, 156
Guernsey Ware China Co. "G.C.Co.," 16
Guernsey Ware, Hotel, 19
Harvest, 141
Hill Craft by Universal, 105
Juvenile Ware, 166
Kitchen Bouquet, 107
Lady Empire (Regency), 125
Leaf Shaped, 110, 150

Mount Vernon, 47
Netherlands, 83
Oakwood, 9
Old Holland Ware, 27
Oxford Ivory, 31
Poppy, 47
Raymor, Golden Burst, 153
Raymor, Sans Souci, 154
Raymor, Shangri-La, 153
Regal-Rochester, 16
Rodeo, 103
Sheffield, 37
The Atlas China Co., 25
Tip Top, 106
Universal Cattail, 144
Upico Ivory, 95
Vogue, 151
Vogue, Stairway to the Stars, 151

Decorations
Alpine, 156
American Beauty Rose, 65, 97
Autumn Fancy, 112
Bamboo, 114
Betsy Rose, 124, 125
Bittersweet, 80, 81
Bouquet, 120
Calico Fruit, 45
Cattail, 56-62, 144
Cherrytone, 42, 43
Circus, 46
Coral Bell, 138
Cottage Garden, 64
Desert Cactus, 54
Echo, 583
Garden Glory, 63, 97
Gloria, 138
Golden Burst, 153
Harvest, 141
Hazelnut, 148
Hollyhock, 48
Indian Tree (Heirloom), 84
Iris, 75, 140
Kitchen Bouquet, 107
Lady Empire, 142
Largo, 111
Maderia, 147

Magnolia, 120
Morning Glory, 140, 150, 156
Moss Rose, 116, 117
Old Curiosity Shop, 38
Park Avenue, 155
Pink Dogwood, 109
Plymouth, 155
Poppy, 47
Rambler Rose, 52
Regency, 125
Rose Corsage, 136
Rose, 127
Roy Rogers, 103
Sans Souci, 154
Shangri-La, 153
Southern Gardens, 134
Stairway to the Stars, 151
Starfire, 121
Starmint, 137
Strawflower, 125
Sweet William, 37
Thistle, 143
Trade Winds, 112
White Peony, 126

Wigwam, 166
Windmill, 44
Wood Hyacinth, 156
Wood Vine, 145

Design

Snowdrop, 22

Nameplates

Baby's Breath, 150
Coral Bell, 138
Echo, 137
Fascination, Plymouth, 155
Gaiety, 168
Moss Rose, 116
Snowdrop, 169
Southern Gardens, 134
Spring Garden, 168
Spring Garden, Mist, 169
Starmint, 137
Strawflower, 135
Sylvan, 169
Trade Winds, 112
White Orchid, 168